"LOVE, LAUGHTER
REV. CHARLE

MW00390036

TABLE OF CONTENTS

DEDICATION

Mom and Dad Charles J. & Marian H. Cummings Sr.,
seen here receiving Holy Communion at my First Mass at
Annunciation Church, Williamsport, Pa.
(the only picture of First Mass May 26, 1968).
To my Brother Jim Cummings and all the family,
I thank you all for your continued love and support.

Annunciation Church   St. Joseph Grade School
Now: St. Joseph Worker   St. John Neumann Reg. Acad.
Parish Community from my Baptism in 1942 to Ordination in 1968

Introduction

At the beginning of my freshman year at Mt. St. Mary's College in Emmitsburg, Md., in 1960, I realized I had to choose my vocation. Like many other young Catholic men growing up in the 1950's, I was considering a religious vocation. After a period of soul-searching and consultation with advisors, I decided to pursue studies for the priesthood. The first hurdle was how to tell my family. I chose to write a letter rather than to tell them face to face. My mother wrote back immediately with this answer: "Your father and I were not surprised at your news and feel that you have chosen correctly, but always remember that this is your decision. If you change your mind we are behind you no matter what you choose to do with your life." My parents and brother Jim Cummings have always been behind me with their support and encouragement.

I wondered, though, whether I was worthy to become a servant of God. Many of the great saints seemed to have struggled with the same question. St. Peter said to Jesus, "Depart from me Lord for I am a sinful man." St Paul willingly acknowledged that he had been a persecutor of the early church, but declared, "It is not I but Christ who lives in me." In his famous classic *Confessions*, St. Augustine wrote of the struggles he underwent before he committed himself to Christianity and the religious life. Even St. Theresa, the Little Flower, in her *Story of a Soul,* indicated her feeling of unworthiness, saying, "So in spite of my littleness, I can hope to be a saint."

Another hurdle for me was the studies. I was never a great student, mediocre at best. To undertake eight years of studying philosophy, church history, Scripture, theology, and Latin, Greek, and Hebrew was a daunting prospect. But my mind was made up. I would accept God's invitation and give myself to the call completely. If I failed along the way, it would be an indication that the priesthood was not my calling.

Before the end of fall in 1960, I wrote a letter with the help of my cousin Fr. Frank Corcoran and Msgr. Frank McHugh, pastor of Annunciation Church, seeking acceptance into the seminary. The Diocese of Scranton advised me to finish my first two years of college and then set up an appointment before the third year of school. In June of 1962 Jerome D. Hannon, then Bishop of the Diocese of Scranton, called me to his office for an interview. He accepted my application and I was to report to St. Pius X Seminary in Dalton, Pa. in September of 1962. I was able to settle into the routine of the seminary life of prayer and study and on May 25, 1968, was ordained a priest for the Diocese of Scranton, Pa., by Bishop J. Carroll McCormick.

After more than 45 years as a priest, my brother Jim Cummings and his son Jim Jr. encouraged me to write some of the stories I had told the family and used in homilies.

A special thanks to my cousin Michael Cummings—former managing editor, reporter and feature writer for the Williamsport *Grit* newspaper and a writing and literature instructor at the Pennsylvania College of Technology. He agreed to edit these stories and make them less wordy and more readable. Let the adventure begins.

St. Pius X Seminary Bishop J. Carroll McCormick, Faculty and Students 1966

My Climb Toward the Priesthood

Ordination to the Diaconate (Sacrament of Holy Orders step one) in May 1967 was the beginning of a banner year in my preparation for the priesthood. I was assigned to St. Mary of the Mount Church in Mt. Pocono to assist Msgr. Connell McHugh, Fr. Bob Galligan, and Fr. John Walsh.

Msgr. McHugh, then 90, was a legend in the Scranton Diocese for his untiring work on behalf of the people of the Pocono Mountains region. Catholics, Protestants, and Jews all loved him. He and the other two priests were responsible for churches in Brodheadsville, Tannersville, Mt. Pocono, Pocono Summit, Cresco, Canadensis, and Promised Land. In addition, the three priests said Sunday Masses resorts at Mt. Airy Lodge, Pocono Manor and a tent in Effort, Pa. In those days, there were no vigil Masses on Saturday evening.

Because there was so much to do and so much territory to cover, four Passionist priests from St. Ann's Monastery in Scranton would come and help out on the weekends.

On Saturday nights, I sat down to supper with all of these priests. It was a gala event, with lots of laughs and stories.

I assisted Fr. Galligan when he said Sunday Mass at three locales: St. Joan of Arc Church in Brodheadsville, a makeshift tent church at Effort, and Mt. Airy Lodge. In his talk at the luxurious Mt. Airy, he would describe the day's ministry as going from "rags to riches" to impress on his well-to-do listeners that "we need your help to continue our mission."

The tent at Effort, about twenty miles from Mt. Pocono, was a real challenge. Because the altar and folding chairs were stored under a tarp next to the main supporting post at the center of the tent, we had to recruit attendees to move the altar to the front and set up the 150 chairs. Before Mass, Fr. Galligan would hear confessions through the window of his car. After Mass, the altar and chairs had to be returned to their storage place beneath the tarp.

One weekday, a parishioner from Effort called to inform me that lightning had struck the main tent post, leaving a huge hole in the tent. When I went over to assess the damage, I discovered that the pole had been splintered into a million pieces. If the congregation had been inside when the lightning struck, there would have been severe casualties. I reported the incident to the Allentown company that erected the tent. The following day, workers from the company cleaned up the mess and erected a new tent. At the next Mass, most parishioners were not aware of what had happened even though splinters littered the area around the tent.

After Mass in the tent, Fr. Galligan would say Mass in Our Lady Queen of Peace Church at Brodheadsville, and I would assist him. In the summers, large crowds would attend—so large on some days that the congregation would spill out the doors and into the yard. One Sunday, I ascended the pulpit of this church to read the Gospel and deliver my first homily as an ordained clergyman. Halfway through my Bible recitation, I realized I was reading the wrong Gospel. Rather than page through the book to find the right Gospel, I decided—in this unnerving moment—to finish reading the wrong Gospel, then deliver the sermon I had prepared. I scolded myself for my stupidity, but all went well and no one threw tomatoes at me.

From the Brodheadsville church, Father Galligan and I would go to Mt. Airy Lodge, which had crystal chandeliers, an outstanding speaker system, uniformed bellmen to act as ushers and take up the collection, and a congregation that often included celebrities. The Mass venue was a large ballroom which, only hours before, had served as a nightclub with a floor show. To prepare for Mass, resort workers would clean the room, clear the clutter, and set up perfect rows of chairs. A professional nightclub pianist would play church hymns for up to three hundred attendees. The liturgy was so well planned and carried out that it was advertised in the resort's brochures.

On weekdays, Fr. Walsh celebrated Masses at St. Mary of the Mount, and I would assist him. Every other day, he allowed me to preach. Between my Sunday and weekday homilies, I received plenty of training that helped diminish my fear of speaking and reading before the public. I am forever grateful for that training.

One time I accompanied Fr. Walsh to a nursing home to assist him in a Holy Communion service. I was to spray mists of holy water around the assemblage while saying a prayer. The bottle of water had a large cap topped with a smaller cap. After removing the smaller cap, one could deliver gentle sprays. But because I was unfamiliar with how the bottle worked, I removed the large cap and drenched the people in several rows with torrents of water. Everyone laughed, including me, and the people went away dripping with holiness.

Msgr. McHugh was a remarkable, kindly man still serving the parish at age 90. The day I arrived at the rectory, he came out to welcome me and to assure me that St. Mary of the Mount was my home as long as I was stationed there.

One evening he asked me to take him to Moosic Lake, where he was to meet Cardinal Patrick A. O'Boyle, Archbishop of Washington, D.C., for supper. There I was, a lowly deacon, who would be hobnobbing with a prince of the church. When we arrived at the lake, Msgr. McHugh gave me $10 and said, "Go get yourself something to eat and pick me up at 9 p.m." My delusions of grandeur about dining with Cardinal O'Boyle were dashed, but I did get to meet the cardinal when I returned to pick up Monsignor.

When I continued to chauffeur Monsignor to various destinations, I asked him one day how long he had been serving in the Poconos. "Father," he said, "I've been here longer than the trees." One thing I learned early on was not to ask him personal questions, such as, "How old are you?" or "How long have you been here?" He didn't want anyone to know anything about him. However, it was obvious from his brogue that he was born in Ireland.

On weekdays before the 8 a.m. Mass, Monsignor would hear confessions, and I was always amazed at the long lines that would form to receive his absolution. After a few weeks of witnessing the long lines, I asked Fr. Walsh why so many people queued up each time Monsignor entered the confessional.

"They all know he's hard of hearing, so they feel comfortable going to confession to him," Fr. Walsh said. "They come from all over the Poconos and even New Jersey to go to confession to him."

Every Saturday night, Msgr. McHugh would leave supper early, then return around 8:30 to join the conversation with the rest of us. One Saturday, Fr. Galligan asked me to take Monsignor's place on one of the outings. The destination was Brookdale on the Lake.

"What am I supposed to do?"

"While people are eating in the dining room," Father Galligan said, "you will get their attention, tell them what a wonderful parish we have here, ask them to help out by buying chances on a car, then go from table to table selling the chances."

I don't think I was ever so embarrassed about something in my life. Msgr. McHugh could charm people with his wit and demeanor and come away with a few hundred dollars. But I, a young deacon interrupting their dinner, could only manage to get a measly $25. I was never again asked to sell chances at Brookdale on the Lake, and I was glad.

The night before my assignment ended at St. Mary of the Mount, I was awakened by knocks on my door. It was Monsignor. "I don't feel well," he said.

Fr. Galligan and I took him to the hospital. He had suffered a heart attack. He recovered somewhat in the ensuing months. However, because of his age and the condition of his heart, he died the following summer, on July 2, 1968.

After the summer at Mt. Pocono I returned to St. Pius X Seminary for my last year of studies. In addition to school, we were assigned to duty in parishes and in my case hospital ministry. Saturday morning I would travel to St. Joseph's Hospital in Hazleton, Pa. My mentor at the hospital was Fr. Thomas Hannigan the hospital chaplain. I was asked to preach the Sunday Mass in the hospital chapel, distribute Holy Communion and visit patients in their rooms. Fr. Hannigan helped me gain experience and appreciate the importance and joy of caring for the sick. I went on to give 15 wonderful years to hospital ministry.

Ordination Day

There I was, one of seventeen men lying prostrate on the floor of the sanctuary of St. Peter's Cathedral in Scranton on Ordination to the Priesthood on May 24, 1968. I and my sixteen colleagues were being made priests of the Scranton Diocese. Our prostration was a symbol of our utter humility before God and our dependence on the prayers of others. It was an unforgettable moment in the Mass, made even more striking by the chanting of the ancient Litany of the Saints.

An interesting footnote to this ordination was that it was taking place on the 100th anniversary of the founding of the Scranton Diocese. More than 100 priests concelebrated the Mass with the principal celebrant, Bishop J. Carroll McCormick. Family members of the ordinands were issued tickets to assure them seats in the overflow crowd. After the Mass, we new priests—sixteen who would serve in the diocese and one who would serve in a religious community—posed for pictures with the bishop on Wyoming Avenue in front of the church, then united with our families for more picture-taking before going home.

I celebrated my first Mass the next day at Annunciation Church in Williamsport at the regularly scheduled 11 a.m. Sunday service. While I was vesting, I felt very nervous—not as much about the ceremony itself but about standing before all my family members and friends. Would they regard me as a real priest with all the faculties required to serve God and his people? As the old saying goes, "A prophet is not without honor except in his native land." That is actually a paraphrase of the words of Jesus: "It is only in his own country, in his own home, and among his own kindred, that a prophet is not honored" (Mark 6:4). These words weighed heavily on my mind that day.

Fr. John Walsh, with whom I had served as a deacon at a church in Mt. Pocono, was the scheduled homilist. He and Annunciation's pastor, Msgr. Frank P. McHugh, were to concelebrate the Mass with me, the principal celebrant. After we put on our vestments, we and the altar servers processed outside the church, from the rear to the front, where we climbed the steps to enter. But an usher had forgotten to unlock the Massive twin front doors. Msgr. McHugh knocked. There was no response. He knocked again with persistence. Still nothing. When he knocked a third time, ushers pushed open a door that almost sent monsignor down the steps. He was okay, though. Meanwhile, the whole incident relaxed me for some strange reason. Then we entered the church and processed up the middle aisle to the altar.

All went well during the Mass. Afterward, everyone attended a reception at a hall at Divine Providence Hospital, which was operated by the Sisters of Christian Charity. It was a wonderful affair. Among those with whom I spoke were friends and relatives I hadn't seen for a long time. At the end of the event, I was exhausted—but joyful and excited.

It was nice to be the center of attention on ordination day and then again on Sunday. On Monday, the SCC Sisters graciously allowed me to say Mass at the hospital chapel. When I emerged from the sacristy, I noticed that about ten people were in the congregation. That was a quick dose of reality. I was not the hot shot I thought I was.

Afterward, one of the sisters asked me to hear the confession of a young nun who was ill. When I entered her room, she was lying in bed, a victim of an affliction that had turned her into an invalid. As I sat in a chair next to her bed, a feeling of inadequacy crept over me. Was I worthy to hear the confession of this young woman patiently enduring her suffering? To have people come to me to pour out their souls in sorrow for their sins was exceedingly humbling. However, to sit before this sister who wanted to dedicate her life to God and to the service of others but who had to accept the heavy cross of sickness and confinement—well, that was even more humbling. Today, almost fifty years later, I continue to be grateful for the opportunity to have served as her confessor. So I had two days of glory and celebration, followed by a third day of reality.

St. Patrick Church Wilkes Barre　　**St. Mary Church Dunmore**
(Asst. Pastor 1968-70)　　　　　　**(Asst. Pastor 1970-74)**

The Stories Begin

1.　The Smile

When I was a young priest, a dying girl taught me a lesson about divine compassion without speaking a word. All she did was smile.

It was 1969. I was an assistant pastor at St. Patrick's Church in Wilkes-Barre, Pa., and a religion teacher at nearby St. Mary's High School. One of my pastoral duties was to visit hospitals in the afternoon or evening to minister to the afflicted.

One morning after class, I did something I had never done before: I skipped my usual coffee klatch with teachers and other priests in the school cafeteria so I could drive to Mercy Hospital in South Wilkes-Barre to see patients. Morning was the worst time to make hospital rounds. Patients were usually undergoing tests, receiving treatment, or conferring with doctors and nurses. Nevertheless, on that morning, something—an intuition, a premonition, a gut feeling—compelled me to go to the hospital.

My first stop was a room on the third floor. There, a girl of about twelve was lying beneath one of those transparent tents used to provide increased oxygen to the lungs and tissues. When she saw me enter, she reached out a hand and smiled. I sat on the side of the bed, raised the oxygen tent, and took her hand. She squeezed it and smiled again, then closed her eyes. Her breathing stopped. Alarmed, I called for help. Nurses entered the room just as the parents were returning from a short break. Moments later, a doctor entered and pronounced her dead.

Along with pastoral counselors from the hospital, I consoled the distraught parents. Although they had known she was about to expire, they were nonetheless devastated after death claimed her. Their shock was normal for a couple that had lost a child to a grave illness.

At the viewing several days later, the parents rushed over to thank me. Thank *me*? What had I done? Then they explained that during her declining days, their daughter prayed constantly that she would not die alone in the dark hours of the night or in the daytime when her mother and father were out of the room. On the morning that she died, nurses were scheduled to come in to bathe her and change her bedclothes. So her parents took the opportunity to get a quick bite to eat. It was when they were out that I entered the room and saw that reaching hand and that smile.

When I took the little girl's hand, apparently God—in his infinite compassion—was answering her prayer not to die alone. But I wonder, during that second smile of hers—that radiant, unforgettable smile—was she looking at me or at the face of her Creator?

2.   The Room Upstairs

Being a hospital chaplain for fifteen years was such rewarding work that I loved every minute of it. The job was not without difficulties and frustrations, however, one of the most trying of which was dealing with patients in extreme chronic pain.

In 1978, I ministered to a cancer patient in excruciating pain the last few weeks of his life. He would writhe in his hospital bed, turning this way and that, over and over again.

At eight o'clock one evening, I was called to see him. On my way to his room, I said a silent prayer: "Please help me, Lord, because I have no idea what to say to him or what to do for him."

He was a widower in his early eighties whose two sisters had cared for him throughout his illness. When I entered his room, one of the sisters asked me to pray with him to take his mind off his pain. After they left, the man told me he was ready to die—sooner rather than later. Before we began to pray, I asked him to do something for me.

"There's a man upstairs who needs to go to confession but is afraid and keeps putting it off," I told him. "Offer your pain for him so God will give him the courage to confess his sins." The widower agreed. We prayed the Our Father together, slowly reciting each word and concentrating on its meaning. Afterward, I administered the sacrament of the sick and absolution, then tried to comfort him as best I could before I left.

At seven the next morning, the hospital switchboard informed me that two messages were awaiting my attention. In the first, time-stamped at 11:05 the previous evening, the cancer patient's sisters told me their brother had died. In the second, time-stamped at 11:08 the previous evening, the "man upstairs" requested that I hear his confession in the morning.

Coincidence? I don't think so.

At the viewing for the cancer patient, the sisters informed me that their brother's pain became more bearable after I left his room. He smiled at them before dying peacefully at 11 p.m. When they inquired about my visit with him, I told them about our prayer session and his willingness to offer his pain for the man who was afraid to confess his sins. Then I told them that within minutes of their brother's death, the other man left a message with the switchboard requesting that I hear his confession.

Offering our pain—whether it is minor or major—for the welfare of another is a noble gesture and a commendable form of prayer. The beneficiary of our suffering can be as far away as a Third World country riddled with disease and famine—or as close as the room upstairs.

3. My Mom's Conversion and the Pope's Gift

When I was growing up more than sixty years ago, the ecumenical movement was already thriving in our Williamsport home. My father was a Catholic, as were my brother Jim and I, but my mother was a Presbyterian. Yet we were a strong, happy family built on Christian foundations.

On Sundays, my mother attended services at Covenant Central Presbyterian Church on West Fourth Street. The rest of us went to Mass at Annunciation Catholic Church about a block away.

After I received my first Holy Communion, Mom started to go to Annunciation with us. One evening at supper in the early fifties, Mom said to Dad, "Someday I would like to talk to Msgr. McHugh [Frank P. McHugh, V. F., pastor of Annunciation Church] about the Catholic faith."

Dad immediately got up from the table and phoned the Annunciation rectory. A moment later, he returned to supper and told my mother that Msgr. McHugh would see her in an hour. She paled, no doubt wondering, *what have I gotten myself into?*

She underwent the required instructions in the faith. Then the time came for her to receive the sacrament of Penance. (Today, we call it the Sacrament of Reconciliation, but most Catholics refer to it as confession.) This is the most difficult sacrament for converts to Catholicism to adjust to.

On her big day, my father said, "Your mother is going to confession for the first time, and we are going with her."

I balked, telling Dad that I had gone to confession just days before with my class at the parish school (St. Joseph's). But he insisted that we receive the sacrament too, saying, "Your mother's a little nervous, so we're going too."

It was a Saturday, the day when most Catholic churches schedule confessions. The lines outside the confessionals were long. My mother's apprehension probably increased as she awaited her turn. Dad was ahead of her and went first. As I recall, he briefed the confessor, Fr. Bernard L. Grogan, assistant pastor, about my mother. All went well that day.

The fact that Mom and Dad took religion so seriously set a good example for me and Jim. Sometimes it's better that way. Homilies are important, but sincerely living one's faith can be just as eloquent as the most skillful preacher.

Msgr. McHugh gave Mom a gift to welcome her into the church: a beautiful crystal rosary. Thereafter, she carried it with her and prayed the rosary faithfully.

One Sunday after we arrived home from Mass, Mom realized that she had left her rosary in church. She and Dad returned to look for it in the pew where we had sat. No luck. We checked the "lost and found" table in the vestibule, but it wasn't there either. Though it wasn't worth much money, the rosary was a cherished treasure to my mother. She was a little disheartened.

Years later, after I became a priest, I spent time in Rome to further my education in a study class with other clergymen. One day, Pope John Paul II spoke to the class in a private audience, then greeted each member individually. When my turn came, I shook hands with the Pope, and he asked me whether my mom was still living. I said yes and he replied, "Here, give this to your mother." It was a small white rosary in a brown packet.

After returning home, I told my mom I had a gift for her. Then I presented her the rosary, saying, "It's from the Pope. He told me to give it to you."

She was thrilled. It remained a closely guarded—and frequently used—treasure of hers for the rest of her life. The times I saw her praying with it were an inspiration to me, as was her courage to follow her heart and convert to Catholicism many years before.

Today, whenever I encounter people thinking about converting to Catholicism, I tell them, "My mother was a convert and I know the struggles you are having." Immediately, barriers fall and they feel comfortable enough to discuss their desire, hesitation, excitement, and fear about adopting a new religion.

So, even though Mom is gone now, her influence on me lives on in my ministry. So does my father's. The example they set for me was their gift to me. The Gospel says, "Let your light shine before men, that they may see your good works, and glorify your Father who is in heaven (Matthew 5:16).

4. Reuniting With Deceased Loved Ones

What if I had been with my two friends when it happened? Would I be dead too?

The three of us were in the fourth grade at St. Joseph's School in my hometown of Williamsport, Pa. One autumn afternoon after school let out early, we walked the short distance to my home on Campbell Street. My mother saw us conferring in front of the house like three explorers plotting their next expedition. Would we climb trees? Play marbles? Hit some baseballs into the stratosphere?

"Don't be late for supper," my mother shouted to me.

My friends, John Bernstine and Michael Clark, had decided on a maritime adventure: a boat ride on the Susquehanna River, which was several blocks south of my house. They coaxed me to come along.

The idea of becoming a Columbus, a Magellan, or even a Blackbeard had its appeal. To leave the shore and ride the waves—ah, me. But dry land also had its appeal, especially since my parents had warned me never to go to the river without adults. So I did something that was hard. I told them, "No thanks," then went inside.

The next morning, my parents summoned me to the breakfast table with the local newspaper spread before them. With solemn voices they informed me that John and Michael had drowned.

I was devastated. And a piercing guilt shot through me. After all, if I had gone with them, I might have been able to talk them out of the boat trip. Of course, it was equally possible that I would have shared in their tragedy.

A few days later, Dad took me to the viewing of each boy. Afterward, I said, "Well, I'll never be with them again for the rest of my life."

My father thought for a moment, then said, "Yes, you will. They're with Jesus now. So the next time you receive Jesus in Holy Communion, all of you will be together."

Those three sentences made up what was probably the best sermon I ever heard, although I didn't realize it at the time.

If we are believers, as I am, we can comfort ourselves in the fact that all those gone from us in death are with us whenever we receive Holy Communion, as my father pointed out. In fact, because they are ever present with Jesus, they are with us even when we pray together in church or at home: "For where there are two or three gathered together in my name," Jesus said, "there am I in the midst of them" (Matthew 18:20).

Now, after a half-century of being priest, I thank my two little friends for being with me when I receive the consecrated Eucharist and then distribute it to members of the congregation so that they, too, can be with their deceased loved ones—so that they, too, can be part of what we Catholics call the Mystical Body of Christ.

What if I had been with John and Michael on that fateful day? I can't answer that question with any certainty. But I can say that I believe God keeps them close to his heart—and that perhaps he kept me away from the river that day because he had a lifelong mission for me to carry out.

5.   Reaching for Heaven

My parents hosted frequent get-togethers at our house on holidays and other special occasions. Guests included aunts, uncles, cousins, grandchildren, and so on.

On one of these occasions in the early 1970s, we were all chattering away in the parlor when my brother, Jim, noticed that his three-old-son, Jimmy, was missing. Alarmed, he conducted a quick search and found the boy in the kitchen standing on a chair pushed up to a cabinet countertop.

He was reaching into a cookie jar. Chocolate icing splotched his face and hands and shirt. His father asked, "What are you doing?" The jig was up, Jimmy realized. But Jimmy was a clever boy, well practiced in the art of exonerating himself from cookie theft and other crimes. He turned to his father and said, "I'm getting a cookie for you, Dad."

His father accepted the gift.

All of us in the other room went to the kitchen to watch as the little thief was cleansed of incriminating evidence and praised for his generosity to his Dad.

Jimmy taught us all a lesson that day: that we should all reach for a little bit of heaven in our daily lives. To a three-year-old, pastries and confections are indeed pieces of heaven. They are for us adults, too—in moderation. But the most important "goody" that we should be reaching for is spiritual nourishment that makes us grow in our faith and eligible to receive the most satisfying goody of all: eternal life with God.

6. That Special Touch

Catholicism evokes images of cavernous churches, stained glass, marble statues, confessionals, and holy water—all familiar hallmarks of the religion. But when I was growing up, I tended to associate Catholicism with Aunt Abby kneeling in a pew—with me next to her.

Aunt Abby was my father's sister. She was one of the millions of ordinary Catholics who undergirded the church in the twentieth century as it preached the Gospel and delivered its message of hope.

When Aunt Abby (Elizabeth K. Cummings) was born in 1895, Mark Twain was still writing books and Wyatt Earp was still riding the range. When she died in 1991, airplanes were flying at triple the speed of sound and a NASA spacecraft was mapping the surface of Venus.

But amid all the changes during her lifetime—including those that flouted religion—Aunt Abby remained steadfast in her faith. Whenever something was going on in the parish church—forty-hours devotions, May crownings, family baptisms and weddings, stations of the cross—she was part of it.

Although she never married, she had scores of children: nephews, nieces, sons and daughters of friends, the paperboy. All of them benefited from her generosity, sometimes coming away from her door with a jingle in a pocket or a bag of freshly roasted peanuts.

She was not wealthy. After all, she was a simple bookkeeper at the local library. But she was unstinting in her support of the church and its mission in the world.

Before my ordination to the priesthood in 1968, I ordered a Gilles Beaugrand chalice of hammered silver plate, along with a paten, from a company in Montreal, Canada. A priest uses a paten and chalice every day at Mass to hold the bread and wine that will be changed during the consecration into the body and blood of Christ, which jointly constitute the Holy Eucharist. It's important for him, therefore, to have durable vessels worthy of holding both elements of the Eucharist.

I was ready to raid my bank account to pay for these vessels when Aunt Abby announced that she would take care of the entire bill, which was considerable. There was no arguing the case. She had made her decision. Years before, she had also paid for the altar vessels of my cousin, the Rev. Frank Corcoran.

After my chalice and paten arrived in the mail, I decided to open the box at the Saturday night supper table, when Aunt Abby would be present. When I placed the chalice in the middle of the table, it reflected the incandescence of our lighting—and the awe on our faces. Aunt Abby reached out a hand, then drew it back.

"Can I touch it?"

Her question reflected the regard she held for sacred objects of the faith. In those days, chalices were usually handled only by the clergy. Even altar boys could not touch them.

But on that evening, I granted Aunt Abby permission to touch the chalice. After all, she had touched me with the good examples she set when I was a boy, examples that helped me decide to become a priest.

There are many Aunt Abbys in the church today, humble people who reflect the light of the Gospels to illuminate the way for the next generation of Catholics.

7. A Christ-like Nun

I was lucky. I had Sister Domitilla in both the first and fourth grades at St. Joseph's School in Williamsport.

She was a young, bespectacled nun who hadn't a cruel bone in her thin body. Yet she was able to manage 72 of us in the first grade (1948-49) and 52 of us in the fourth (1951-52). There were no teacher aides to help her and no technical devices to ease her task. During bathroom and playground breaks, she was always nearby to monitor us.

Under Sister Domitilla, I learned to read well enough to peruse the Gospels. I also mastered enough arithmetic to calculate the perimeter of a ham sandwich and the circumference of a basketball.

Perhaps her most memorable trait was her kindness. In a day when some teachers in private and public schools wielded paddles and wooden rods to discipline students, Sister Domitilla used smiles and gentle words. And she succeeded!

One morning in the fall of 1951, we fourth-graders received terrible news. Two of our classmates—John Bernstine and Michael Clark—had drowned in the Susquehanna River the previous day after going out in a boat without adult supervision. The newspaper headline about their deaths shocked the entire community. In those days, our school remained in session after such tragedies. No psychologists or psychiatrists came to counsel students.

When Sister Domitilla entered our classroom at the beginning of the school day, 50 bewildered kids confronted her with questions.

"Will we ever see John and Michael again?"

"Will God punish them for taking the boat out without permission?"

"Why didn't their guardian angels save them?"

"Will our sadness ever go away?"

Sister Domitilla answered all of our questions. I can't remember how apt or appropriate her answers were, but I can say that most of us—as far as I could tell—felt a tad better at the end of the day. We were able to climb out of the nightmare, pray for the repose of the souls of John and Michael, then go home and do what kids do: play hopscotch, ring-around-the rosie, and hide-and-seek. To be sure, there was a dark recess in our minds that presented images of the tragedy. But there were also the comforting words of Sister Domitilla stroking our brains.

About 40 years later, I ran into Sister Domitilla in Scranton when I was serving there as a priest. I was astounded that she remembered me. When we talked about old times, she said she remembered that awful day in 1951, when John and Michael died. She told me that helping our fourth-grade class to cope with the tragedy was the most difficult moment of her life as a nun.

I'll wager that it was also her most Christ-like moment.

8. Rude Awakening

When I was stationed at Our Lady of Mt. Carmel Parish in Dunmore in 1974, a terrible crash awakened me one morning in my upstairs bedroom at the rectory. It was around 7 o'clock. I guessed that a person or an animal had bulled through a downstairs window or one of the large glass panels on either side of the front door.

While another priest in the rectory called the police, I hurried down the steps and encountered a man standing in shards of glass. He was bleeding from a hand wound he had suffered when he broke through one of the panels.

"I want to see Msgr. Larkin," he said.

Msgr. Raymond Larkin, the former church pastor, had moved to Villa St. Joseph in Dunmore, a home for retired diocesan priests. After I told the intruder that Msgr. Larkin no longer lived in the rectory, he turned around and stepped through the space occupied by the panel minutes before, trailing blood behind him.

Meanwhile, the police arrived at the very moment that a third priest stationed at the parish was saying the 7 o'clock Mass in the church, St. Mary of Mount Carmel. After they spotted a man walking toward the church entrance, they drew their guns and pinned him against a car. By this time, I was outside, observing, dressed only in my pajamas. When I realized that the suspect in custody was a parishioner—a fellow who had arrived late for Mass—I ran across the lawn and told the police that they had the wrong man, then pointed them in the direction of the trail of blood. They released the parishioner and hightailed it after the intruder.

A short time later, they returned to the rectory and told us the intruder had been taken to a hospital for treatment of his wound. He had escaped from Clark Summit State Hospital for the mentally ill, the police said, and would be returned there unless we wanted to press charges. Because of his mental disability, we decided that the state hospital—not a jail—was the best place for him.

What an unfortunate creature he was, I thought, and I knew it was my duty to pray for him. Did he have a purpose in the world? I believe he did, although I could not then—and cannot now—identify it.

After the great English poet John Milton (1608-1674) lost his eyesight, he thought his life was over—that he had no purpose anymore. Later, however, he realized that everyone had a purpose, regardless of his or her flaws or infirmities. Then he sat down and wrote this immortal line in one of his sonnets: "They also serve who only stand and wait."

9. A Silent Sermon

Although paralysis had robbed Molly's arms and legs of their ability to move, she could smile and talk. I call her Molly because privacy restrictions prevent me from revealing her real name.

Molly was a patient in a Williamsport nursing home that I visited frequently in the early 1980s to distribute Holy Communion. Staff members had to feed and bathe her, prop her up, and provide whatever other care she required. Sometimes, they moved her from her bed to a chair for a change of scenery.

Molly's limitations did not stop her from living a full and fruitful life. For example, she spent several hours a day reading books and magazines on a stand positioned before her, using a rubber-tipped wand clenched in her mouth to turn the pages. Her reading enabled her to inform herself on the issues of the day, entertain herself with intriguing stories, and travel the world on the wings of an author's imagination. She also prayed at least two or three hours every day, saying the rosary, mouthing the words in prayer books, or meditating on a religious theme or image.

Whenever friends or relatives stopped by, she beamed a welcoming smile and asked about their health, their families, their jobs, and so on. Before long, these visitors were telling her about their troubles. She would listen intently, never interrupting but always radiating love and concern. Having emptied themselves of their burdensome thoughts, they would go away from her feeling better.

I was among those who benefited from her hearkening ear. Too often, though, I neglected to ask her how she was doing before I left.

Nurses would marvel at her extraordinary patience, dignity, and holiness.

Whenever difficulties invade my life, I think of this remarkable woman and the suffering she endured uncomplainingly, all the while exhibiting joy and serenity. My difficulties then seem small by comparison.

Molly's life was a silent sermon. With her smile, her optimism, and her faith in God, she must have inspired many people without saying a word.

10. A Prayerful Woman

Members of St. Mary's Parish in Dunmore exhibited such devotion to the Holy Eucharist when I was stationed there in 1974 that we priests (the pastor, myself, and another assistant) had over one hundred First Friday communion calls. Our mail man would walk in one door of the church and out the other. I asked him one day, "Gene, why do you walk through the church?" He said, "Just stop to say hello to the Lord."

One of my communicants was a happy and delightful woman who lived alone in a first-floor apartment with a door that opened to the street. Her husband was deceased, and her children were all grown and living out of town. But she had lots of friends. Because she kept her door unlocked on most days, any of these friends could walk right in and enjoy her company. She was a reliable source of news about parishioners who were sick or in need.

This woman spent many hours each day saying the rosary or praying from books and cards. On a side table were holy cards neatly arranged in eight or ten little stacks.

One day I asked her, "Why are these cards lined up in a row?"

"That's 9 o'clock," she said, pointing to a stack. "The next one's 10 o'clock, the one after that is 11 o'clock, and so on."

Amazing, I thought. Each hour she is lifting her mind and heart to God just as monks and nuns do in monasteries and convents.

Out of curiosity, I asked her, "What if you make a mistake and say the 9 o'clock prayers at 10 o'clock?"

"Oh, that's okay, Father," she replied. "Jesus knows that it's the thought that counts."

The lesson for me was that it is not WHAT you pray but THAT you pray. Later, I made up a little poem to remind myself of the importance of this lesson.

Just Pray

It doesn't matter what I pray. It doesn't matter when I pray.
It doesn't matter where I pray. It doesn't matter why I pray.
It doesn't matter how I pray.   *   It only matters THAT I pray.

11. A Stubborn Woman

When I was stationed in Wilkes-Barre, I took Holy Communion one winter morning to a parishioner living in one side of a double house that she owned. No tenants occupied the other side.

She was sick and could not care for the house or herself. Consequently, her half of the double was a mess, with paper and trash in every corner. In the room where she was living, she burned Sterno to provide warmth. Worried that she might set the house on fire, I asked her to let me call someone to help her.

"Absolutely not," she said. "No one is going to come and tell me what to do or take me from my home."

Nevertheless, I reported her plight to the office of public assistance. However, its representatives told me they already knew about this woman but could not intervene. Because she owned the home and was not endangering her neighbors, they could not legally act on her behalf unless she requested help.

"In order to forcibly help her," they said, "we must have her declared incompetent and, by court order, remove her from the home."

I felt helpless. Because she was not incompetent, court action was out of the question. The problem was that she stubbornly refused help of any kind. No doubt she feared losing control over her life and her home.

From time to time, priests encounter woeful situations like hers and bureaucratic systems that offer no solutions. It's frustrating. In our country, the freedom to be stubborn is a right even when doing so is wrong.

Some days have happy endings. Some do not.

This much I can say for the woman, though: she did not forget about God.

12. Seeing the Light

One man felt blessed. The other felt cursed. They were both in their early eighties. Each had a wonderful family with a devoted wife and many children. And each was scheduled to undergo open heart surgery at Mercy Hospital in Scranton. They shared the same hospital room, with curtains drawn around their beds.

The year was 1988, when I was the hospital's Catholic chaplain. It was my custom to visit newly admitted patients right after supper.

After I drew back a curtain, I greeted the first man and began chatting with him.

"Father," he said, "I have been a very fortunate man. I have a loving wife, five great kids who are doing well, and many grandchildren. Until my retirement, I had a rewarding job that I really liked. If God takes me tomorrow, if I don't make it through this operation, I have no regrets since I've been so blessed."

I gave him the Sacrament of the Sick and Holy Communion, then assured him I would pray for his health and healing at daily Mass in the hospital chapel.

After I looked in on the other man, I heard a different story.

"You know, Father, I can't figure it out. I have a good wife, six children who make me proud, and many wonderful grandchildren. I had a good job, too. I have always gone to church and brought up my kids in the church and tried to be a good example to them. *Now* look. I am lying here sick, flat on my back. Why is God punishing me?"

He then confessed his sins, and I gave him the Sacrament of the sick and Holy Communion. Before I left, I told him God was not punishing him in any way.

"God loves us all," I said, "and gives us the grace to face the struggle of illness."

Both men came through the surgery well and went on to live many more years. My experience with them left me wondering why the second man dwelt on the dark clouds in an otherwise bright sky while the first man saw only the sun and the blue. I'll leave that for psychologists to explain.

However, it's good for all of us to keep in mind what Jesus said: "I am the light of the world. . . . He who follows me can never walk in darkness; he will possess the light of life" (John 8:12).

13. Deep Regret

The Catholic Church regards willful abortion as one of the most serious sins. But can a woman guilty of this sin receive absolution immediately in the confessional if she is truly sorry for her transgression?

Yes!

Thanks to changes which have been approved, a contrite woman today can confess this sin in the privacy and secrecy of the confessional and go away with the assurance that God has cleansed her soul of all stain of mortal sin.

However, we priests at one time had to ask a bishop to approve remittance of the sin of abortion. I vividly remember one woman who confessed this sin in my confessional before the changes took effect. She was very upset and deeply penitent and contrite. To console her, I told her that Our Lord forgives her sins. However, I also informed her that I had to receive the bishop's permission to give her absolution. I instructed her that all she had to do was return to my confessional the following week. By that time, I would have the proper faculties to proceed with absolution.

"Please don't worry," I told her. "This requirement is imposed on me and in no way challenges your sincerity or your worthiness to receive God's forgiveness."

She assured me she would return in a week. But she never came back.

To this day, I regret not applying a rule of Canon Law called "ecclesia supplet" ("the church supplies"). In effect, it means that the church will validate an action even if certain conditions have not been met. Maybe that rule did not apply in this woman's case. Nevertheless, if I had told the woman I was using it, she would have gone from the confessional feeling forgiven. Instead, she never returned, and I pray that she did not carry the burden of sin for the rest of her life because of the rigidity of that particular rule placed on us in the private confines of the confessional.

Today, under the changes a priests can absolve the sin of abortion immediately. Perhaps the church changed the law because so many women who were contrite and penitent were afraid to return to the confessional to receive absolution.

14. The Orphan

When I was attending Mount St. Mary's College in Emmitsburg, Md., its 1,200 male students had the opportunity to join clubs and other organizations to work for the betterment of the less fortunate.

One of the organizations that I joined arranged for students to spend time at a Catholic orphanage a short distance to the north, across the border with Pennsylvania. It was operated by the Diocese of Harrisburg. This was a time (the early 1960s) before foster care became the norm.

On weekends, we students would go up to the orphanage to play baseball, basketball, soccer, and other games with the kids. It was an enjoyable time not only for the children but also for us. Students from St. Joseph's College, an all-female school in Emmitsburg, would also visit the orphanage on weekends to play games with the girls.

As my Mount St. Mary's group was preparing to return to the college one Saturday afternoon, one of the boys came up to me and said, "My name is Cummings, too—Dennis Cummings. Do you think your family would let me come to live with them?"

How do you explain to a seven-year-old that you don't live at home anymore? How do you explain that you are in college and couldn't possibly take him home with you?

I was crushed to leave that afternoon and see that little boy left behind. I was crushed to see all of those children left behind to live in an institution without the love and security of a family. I'll never forget the forlorn look on that little boy's face as we drove away. What pain so many children must bear.

15. Awakening to Christ

You never know what to expect when you say Mass in a nursing home. Some attendees may begin talking out loud or cursing. Others may become sick or get up and walk around the room. I always ask the staff to try to make sure that residents planning to attend Mass are alert and able to follow along during the service.

At one nursing home where I had previously said Mass, I was preparing all the necessities for the Eucharistic celebration when I saw a man in the congregation who looked familiar to me. I asked an attendant who he was. She told me his name was Ang and that he once was a parishioner at a church where I was stationed. But Ang did not acknowledge my greeting and did not seem to recognize me. He was in his own little world.

Memories of him and his wife quickly came back to me. They were the kind of parishioners every pastor longs for. Not only were they devout, attending daily Mass often, but they were also very helpful. They cleaned the church and did repairs, worked in the kitchen, distributed church bulletins, took up collections, and did various other odd jobs. After Ang's wife died, he eventually ended up in the nursing home after finding it difficult to get along on his own.

After completing my preparations for Mass, I began the opening prayer, saying loudly, "In the name of the Father, and of the Son, and of the Holy Spirit." Looking up, Ang suddenly came to life and said just as loudly, "Amen." As Mass progressed, he remained alert and continued to respond appropriately to every prayer. He received Holy Communion with great reverence, as he had always done as a parishioner. When the Mass ended, he looked up at me and said, "Thanks for coming, Fr. Cummings."

It so happened that the Gospel for the Mass on that day was about the encounter between Jesus and two of his disciples on the evening of the day of his resurrection. The disciples were walking to the village of Emmaus while discussing the events of the previous two days. Jesus appeared and joined them in their walk, but they did not recognize him.

Later, when they invited him to supper with them at Emmaus, he remained a stranger to them. "And then, when he sat down at table with them, he took bread, blessed and broke it, and offered it to them; whereupon their eyes were opened, and they recognized him; and with that, he disappeared from their sight" (Luke 24:30-31).

It was in the breaking of the bread that they recognized Jesus. And, apparently, it was when I began Mass and later read the Gospel that Ang emerged from his little world and regained his memories of me, of the Mass, and of the resurrected Jesus as retold in Luke's Gospel.

I stayed for a while and we talked and got reacquainted. When I told him of my amazement at his sudden awakening at Mass, he simply explained that he just drifted off like that from time to time, making him oblivious of what was happening around him.

Let us keep our attention on the breaking of the bread, and to the hope of salvation it offers.

16. Memorable Thursday

After confessing my sins, I forgot the words to the Act of Contrition.

Now what?

It was the first Thursday of September 1952, when I was a ten-year-old student at St. Joseph's School in Williamsport. The nuns had just marched our class to the parish church for confession to prepare us to receive Holy Communion the next day, First Friday.

First Friday was a special occasion, dedicated to the Sacred Heart of Jesus. To receive God's graces on the First Friday of any month, we needed to attend Mass and receive the Eucharist. In those days, we had to fast from midnight until we received communion. After Mass, we ate breakfast in the school at our desks. Because church law forbade eating meat on Fridays, our sandwiches were usually spread with egg salad or a tuna concoction. We washed the food down with half a pint of white or chocolate milk.

Anyway, on that memorable September Thursday, three priests were waiting to hear our confessions in the church: two assistant pastors in enclosed confessionals in the back of the church and the pastor, Msgr. Frank P. McHugh, seated on a chair behind a screen mounted on the altar rail. I preferred Msgr. McHugh because he was such a kind man, a grandfatherly figure to me. I remember elbowing, begging, bribing, or doing whatever else it took to get into his line.

When my turn came, I knelt at the altar rail and recited, "Bless me, Father, for I have sinned," then confessed my transgressions. When it was time for me to recite the Act of Contrition to affirm my penitence, my mind went blank. There was a pause. Then I said, "Uh, oh, Father, I can't remember the words."

Patiently Msgr. McHugh said, "O my God—" I repeated the phrase. Then he said, "I am heartily sorry—" Again I repeated the phrase. He led me through the whole prayer a few words at a time without a hint of impatience. After I recited the final words of the prayer, he said, "You know, if you say this prayer every night before you go to sleep, you will never forget it."

What a beautiful lesson to give a young child. Monsignor did not scold me but encouraged me to pray the Act of Contrition often so that I would remember it. He was right. From that day forward, I have prayed the Act of Contrition every night before I go to sleep and have never forgotten it.

17. A Noteworthy Confession

St. Patrick's Church in Wilkes-Barre is a cavernous building with a dome visible for miles around. Before I celebrated my first Mass there, the pastor warned me to speak slowly and distinctly. Otherwise, my words would become mumbles after echoing around the dome and off the walls.

After several Masses and homilies, I learned to speak at just the right speed. Unfortunately, though, one young husband and wife never heard a word I said. Let me explain.

One Saturday afternoon when I was hearing confessions, a hand poked into the confessional and presented a note with a list of sins and these instructions: "Please write my penance on the paper and forgive my sins." Did this note mean that the penitent was too timid to confess aloud? Did the penitent have a speaking or hearing impairment?

Whatever the reason, it didn't matter. I had no pen or pencil.

When I stepped outside the confessional to confer with the person, I discovered that it was a man who was totally deaf. So was his wife, who was next in line with her own list.

I motioned for them to come to the sacristy with me. There, I did my best to make them comfortable. After conducting the penitential rite for each of them, I wrote down their penances, gave them absolution, and returned their notes.

After a time, they came to the rectory for confession. Meanwhile, I began to study sign language to communicate with them. Whenever I struggled with my uneducated hands to greet them or discuss news of the day, they waited patiently without criticizing me. Sometimes I signed a word or a concept that left them dumbfounded. Still they remained polite. Then came the day when we all burst out laughing at my ineptitude. Fortunately, they could read my lips when I spoke to them as they faced me.

It can be a great challenge for a priest to communicate with the deaf, but I found that just trying is very much appreciated. There are similar difficulties with those who stammer and those who struggle with speech impairments resulting from cerebral palsy, stroke, or another affliction.

We priests should never ignore or neglect persons with speech or hearing impairments. Instead, we should do everything in our power to communicate with them.

18. The Empty Church That Was Full

When I and four other altar boys arrived about ten minutes before the funeral, the church was empty. Not a single person sat in the pews. Were people staying away because the deceased had committed a heinous crime?

It was a school day in the early 1950s. We altar boys had been summoned from class at St. Joseph's School to serve the funeral Mass at the parish church, Annunciation. "Serving" a Mass meant reciting prayer responses in Latin, presenting bread and wine to the priest, ringing bells at the consecration, assisting the priest when he distributed communion to the congregation, and performing various other tasks.

But at this funeral Mass, there was no congregation. Besides those of us in the sanctuary, the only attendees were the funeral director and six other men who had volunteered to be pall bearers. Msgr. Frank P. McHugh, the pastor, presided at the funeral.

Afterward, we altar boys asked monsignor why no one but the funeral director and pall bearers occupied the pews during Mass. He explained that the deceased was a very old woman from a nursing home, so old that she had outlived all her family members, relatives, and friends.

How sad it was, we boys thought, that no familiar faces had surrounded this woman when she was dying. But monsignor told us that she did have family members present at the funeral—us—as members of the mystical body of Christ. Monsignor did not go into detail about the meaning of the mystical body, but we got the message.

Later, I reviewed a section on the mystical body in a book used by most Catholic schoolchildren in the mid-twentieth century, the Baltimore Catechism. It said that the mystical body (sometimes referred to as "the communion of saints") was a family consisting of faithful church members on earth, the souls of the deceased in heaven, and the souls earning heaven with their suffering in purgatory. All were united with Christ as the head of the mystical body.

In other words, we altar boys were, in fact, members of the deceased woman's family. And so was Christ himself!

Who can say that He was not there, in a pew—along with all the other members of the mystical body, including the elderly woman's relatives and friends—during the funeral?

19. A Mouse With a Mission

Lord forgive us, but some of us priests think we spellbind our parishioners with our sermons. So we go on, and on, and on. Although I always try to stop talking before the first yawn in the congregation, I have to admit I wasn't always short-winded.

In 1974, when I was a young priest at St. Mary's Church in Dunmore, I passed the yawning point one Sunday morning in my sermon at the 7 a.m. Sunday Mass. The moment came when I noticed that all eyes in the pews had shifted away from me.

Was my sermon that tedious?

Then I noticed that the parishioners' gazes were fixed on the maroon curtain behind the main altar. The congregation was quiet, but some people were elbowing one another and pointing.

Was it an apparition?

Out of curiosity I turned around and saw a mouse performing daredevil antics on the velvet surface of the curtain. Up, up he would go—to the very top—then across, then down, then back up. For a change of pace, he ran in circles. Round and round he would go and when he would stop nobody knew.

How could I compete with this vaudevillian? Quickly, I wrapped up the sermon and moved on to the other parts of the Mass. But the mouse continued to ramble, like a long sermon, and kept it up until the end of Mass.

The little pipsqueak! I had seen him the night before after hearing confessions. When I chased him up an aisle, he disappeared into some nook or cranny—then waited patiently to disrupt my sermon the next day. And he did the same thing to other priests at the rest of the Sunday Masses.

The pastor wasn't amused, and we declared war on the mouse. Baited traps were set, and the janitor kept a broom at the ready. The mouse took the bait, but the guillotine failed to fall. Over the next two weeks, he performed encore performances during Mass. Up he would go, then down, then around. Sometimes he ran under the pews to terrorize the parishioners.

One day, he disappeared and never returned.

Someone theorized that a hidden trap had snared him. Another thought a belfry bat had consumed him. Here's what I think. The mouse moved to another church to disrupt long sermons; that was his mission in life.

I know this much: he succeeded with me. Ever since that time, I have always stopped preaching at the yawning point. Well, almost every time.

20. Overcoming Adversity

When I was serving at St. Patrick's Church in Wilkes-Barre, I was privileged to work with a young woman who exemplified a memorable Bible passage: "Affliction gives rise to endurance" (Romans 5.3).

To guard her identity, I'll call her Margaret. She was a victim of cerebral palsy, a cruel disorder with a long list of symptoms. In general, it affects movement, coordination, balance, and posture to varying degrees. Muscles become rigid or flaccid and bones may be deformed. The victim may suffer tremors and seizures, as well as vision and speech problems. Some patients struggle with impaired intellectual skills. Usually, the symptoms are permanent.

Margaret's symptoms confined her to a wheelchair and robbed her of the ability to speak clearly. If she wanted to write a message instead of speaking it, she could not. The affliction had taken away her ability to form letters.

Nevertheless, Margaret bore up under her burdens, thanks to her dedicated family, strong will and faith in God. In fact, she did more than bear up; she embraced the challenges before her.

She was among those whom the priests of St. Patrick's ministered to at a local activity center for CP victims. Once a week, I would visit the center to give short talks, answer questions, and hear confessions. Once a month, I would say Mass there.

In those days, many of the adults at the center had never attended school because the public regarded them as retarded. Margaret, however, knew she had a sharp mind and proved it by graduating from high school. Even more, she attended Wilkes University, where she was a student when I met her. She recorded the lectures and progressed at her own pace, adjusting her workload whenever necessary.

Her fellow students, amazed at her spunk and derring-do, cheered her on. No doubt she inspired them to be better students—and human beings. Whenever I conducted a religious activity at the center, she was there. She attended all of my Masses. I noticed, however, that she never received Holy Communion. When I asked her why, she said that others—including another priest—had told her, "You don't need to go to communion." Perhaps they thought she had swallowing difficulties, as some CP victims do. I then asked her whether she wanted to receive communion.

"Absolutely," she replied.

Because she was a faithful Catholic who attended church regularly with her family, I saw no reason to deny her the Eucharist. At the center the following week, we had a beautiful celebration of the Mass at which she received her first Holy Communion with her family and friends in attendance. Also attending were all the members of the center's CP group and all the staff members. It was a moving experience for everyone.

I was told that Margaret went on to graduate from Wilkes, a distinction in itself considering her difficulties. She had exhibited the endurance and perseverance to climb an Everest, with the help of God and her wonderful family. When I left St. Patrick's and moved on to another assignment, I took my memory of this young woman with me. Whenever I need to confront my own challenges, this memory props me up. And, when I tell others about her, it heartens them to face their challenges.

21. The Rescue

When I knocked on the front door, there was no response. I was on my First Friday rounds taking Holy Communion to shut-ins.

I knocked again, then pounded. But the old woman inside the big house still failed to respond. At the time, the early 1970s, I was serving at St. Mary's Church in Dunmore with two other priests. On First Fridays, all three of us would take the Eucharist to parishioners confined to their homes.

The woman inside was in her nineties. She was a pleasant, prayerful woman who got along well on her own. A daughter who lived nearby lent her a helping hand whenever she needed it.

I knocked one more time. Still no response. I began peeking through windows. From a side porch, I saw what looked like two legs sticking out from beneath the table in the dining room. Immediately, I called the police. Minutes later, an officer arrived and broke the window of the kitchen door with a club. We entered and went to the dining room.

"Thank God you arrived, Father," the woman said. "I thought I was going to die lying on the floor."

She had been in that position for a whole day after taking a fall. Her daughter, attracted by the sound of the police car's siren, entered the house just then with a look of alarm. But she was relieved when she saw that her mother was alive and conscious. We called an ambulance. Doctors in the emergency room said she had broken a hip. After undergoing surgery, she made a complete recovery while recuperating in the hospital and later a nursing home. Able to fend for herself again, she returned to her residence.

God must have been with her that morning when she was lying on the floor and praying for help, for a door was opened unto her—with the help of a policeman's club.

22. My Incredible Golf Drive

It was a wondrous spring morning in the mid-1960s. The sun was bright, the dew glistened, and the fragrance of lilacs wafted in the breeze. I was with my cousin, Mike, at the White Deer Golf Course, about seven miles south of Williamsport. We were full of anticipation and optimism, as most golfers are when they step up to the first tee. There would be many pars, perhaps a birdie or two, and—who knew?—even a hole in one. Or so we dreamed.

In the car on the way to the golf course, my cousin had told me about his golf outing the previous week with a friend. On the first hole, he hit the ball straight and long—at least 250 yards, he said. He thought the shot was a harbinger of a record-setting round as he walked toward the ball. Then a groundhog sallied forth from trees on the left side of the fairway, scooped the ball into its mouth, and returned to the trees.

As we pulled into White Deer, he asked, "What does the rule book say about acts of nature like that?" I couldn't answer that question, but I did tell him that there were rules covering strange situations. For example, according to *Golf Digest*, if a ball stops next to a cactus, you can wrap a towel around your arm to protect it from the cactus needles as you swing. The same source said that if a ball comes to rest inside a clubhouse that is in bounds, you must play the ball. You are allowed to open a window or door to hit the ball back onto the fairway.

My cousin said, "What about groundhogs?"

I had no answer for him. But I did tell him about "the burning bush." That's a well-documented story about golfers playing a parched course in an Arizona desert. After one player hit his ball out of the rough, the dry grass and bushes around him burst into flames. His playing partners had to beat at the burning bushes with towels and golf bags to rescue him. Apparently, the player's metal club head had glanced off a stone, causing a a spark.

Anyway, at White Deer, we flipped a coin to see who would go first. As we did so, I noticed dark storm clouds gathering ominously on the western horizon. The wind had picked up.

"Maybe the storm will blow over," I said.

My cousin won the coin toss. He kissed his golf ball, teed up, and swung from the heels. The ball rocketed straight ahead for a moment, then curved left and landed out of bounds—in the same spot to which the groundhog had taken his ball the previous week. He stepped back, inspected the head of his driver, and mumbled something to it.

I stepped up and perched my ball on the tee. It sat there fat and sassy, awaiting a mighty blow. Although the wind had quickened even more, a shaft of sunlight broke through the dark clouds, perhaps to spotlight me. It was a good omen. When I swung, my club head went too far beneath the ball and I took a divot. That was not supposed to happen with a driver. I must have slipped on the dewy ground. Or maybe my driver was bent. Whatever the case, the ball rose almost vertically. And then it happened. A gust of wind—one might say a great wind, one might even say a biblical wind—rushed eastward, blowing the ball behind me. I had lost about twenty yards. What does the rule book say about hitting a ball backward? Several other golfers waiting to tee off began chuckling.

My cousin and I both decided to take mulligans and allow the smart alecs to play through. We then teed off anew. At the end of the day, our scores were biblical, in the Methuselah range, requiring an Einstein to calculate.

I went away wondering what the distance record was for hitting a golf ball backward. It was possible that I owned that record.

23. Smelling Smoke

The human nose can distinguish more than a trillion smells, according to *Science*, a weekly journal. It published an article on this topic on March 21, 2014.

Thank God for the nose.

Without it, we wouldn't be able to appreciate the fragrance of flowers or the aroma of freshly brewed coffee. And I wouldn't have been able to forestall disaster at the rectory of St. Mary of Mount Carmel Church in Dunmore in 1971. At the time, I was the youngest of four priests stationed there. The others were Msgr. Joseph Quinn, the pastor; Msgr. Raymond Larkin, the retired pastor; and the Rev. William Healey, an assistant pastor. The rectory was relatively new, built in the sixties to replace its dilapidated predecessor.

Msgr. Larkin, who was in his early eighties, was biding his time at the rectory while the diocese was completing a new retirement home for priests, Villa St. Joseph, also in Dunmore. But he was still active, still celebrating Mass and helping out whenever we needed a hand.

One Sunday afternoon in the summer, I was watching a baseball game on television when I smelled smoke. Msgr. Larkin, who was in his living quarters watching TV, was an avid cigar smoker. But what I smelled wasn't tobacco smoke. It was something different. Starting with the cellar, I checked for signs of fire. Nothing. Working my way up through the rectory to the roof, I went from room to room, inspecting every nook and cranny. Still nothing. The only place I hadn't checked was Msgr. Larkin's apartment. I knocked on the door.

"Come in," he said with a welcoming tone.

When I entered, a thick cloud of smoke greeted me. Msgr. Larkin was puffing away on a perfecto, as usual, with his gaze fixed on the TV. But I knew that he could not have generated the billowing cloud enveloping the room no matter how much he loved his cigar.

"Monsignor, something's on fire," I said. "You've got to get out of here."

"I wondered why I couldn't see the TV anymore," he replied nonchalantly.

As it turned out, the motor on the fan he was using had caught fire. I unplugged the fan, took it outside, and then opened a window to clear the smoke.

It's a good thing our noses are smart enough to detect the difference between cigar smoke and the smoke produced by a burning motor. Thank God.

24. The Persistent Prayer

For more than 50 years, she prayed daily for her brother. And then one day her petition was granted.

When she was born in Ralston, Pa., on Aug. 4, 1888, her parents— Mr. And Mrs. Constantine Gallagher—named her Ellen Irene. She was the youngest of eight children. Her mother, whose maiden name was Elizabeth Jane Cummings, was the sister of my grandfather.

In January 1909, Ellen Irene went to Scranton and entered the convent of the Sisters, Servants of the Immaculate Heart of Mary (IHM). Thereafter, she was known as Sister Mary Dunstan.

When Ellen Irene was only a year old, her father died. Mrs. Gallagher, who had no means of support, then moved with her children to the farmstead of her mother's family in nearby Cascade Township. It was not uncommon in those days for a family enduring hard times to take up residence with relatives. After all, there was no organized welfare system, no public assistance. But the Gallaghers survived, like the birds of the air in Matthew's Gospel (6:26).

The Gallagher children attended a one-room school. After class, they learned the meaning of hard work on the farm where they lived.

One day in 1908, after her mother died, Ellen Irene—an intelligent, sensitive young woman—announced to her brothers and sisters that she planned to enter the IHM convent in Scranton. One of her brothers objected vehemently. There was work to be done. How could she abandon the family? How could she throw her life away on such foolishness? If she went through with her plans, he said, he would never again speak to her and never again go to church.

But the call of God was strong within her, and she left. Afterward, her brother was good to his word. He cut off all contact with his sister and stopped going to church.

Meanwhile, Sister Mary Dunstan took up her calling with enthusiasm, serving as an educator in Pittston, Pa.; Forest Hills, N.Y.; and Pittsburgh. She went on to become a highly respected principal at three schools, one in Edgewood, R.I, and the other two in Olyphant and Archbald, near Scranton.

All the while—even from her first day in the convent, Jan. 6, 1909—she prayed fervently for her brother, asking God to reunite her with him and bring him back to the church. She never gave up hope, never slackened in her petitions to the Lord. One day, she received word that her brother was in a hospital with a serious illness and wanted to see her. Immediately, she went to him. There, in his hospital bed, he apologized to his sister, imploring her to forgive him for his hardness of heart and all the pain he had caused her over the years. Then he asked her to contact a priest to hear his confession and give him the last rites, a term once used for the Sacrament of the Sick. He died in 1960, reconciled with his sister and with his church.

St. Matthew's Gospel says, "Ask, and it shall be given you: seek, and you shall find: knock, and it shall be opened to you" (7:7). Sister Mary Dunstan asked, then asked again and again. Eventually, the Gospel promise was fulfilled.

When we pray, we don't know when and how God will answer us. But the door is always open, and He is always listening.

25. The Vow

When I was an assistant pastor at St. Mary's Church in Dunmore, one of our parishioners had a severe alcohol problem. The community referred to him as "the town drunk."

One day he arrived at the rectory in a cab. When he got out of the car, he was so drunk that the driver had to help inside.

"I want to take the pledge," he said.

Alcoholics often vow to give up drink in a state of inebriation, then go right back to drinking after they sober up. Nevertheless, I typed out a pledge: "I solemnly swear that I will never take another drink." He signed it with trembling hands and, for good measure, spoke the words of the pledge. As the driver was helping him out the door, he whispered to me, "He has a whole bottle of booze in the cab." I paid the driver and asked him to take the man home.

The next day, the man attended the 7 a.m. Mass, sober but a bit shaky. He asked to go to confession, and I obliged him. He continued to attend daily Mass with no visible signs of drunkenness. Skeptics probably suspected him of taking a nip now and then. However, he would always tell the priest who said Mass, "Another day without a drink, Father." I think we priests at the morning Mass were the equivalent of his daily AA meeting. After he kept coming to Mass and reporting to us, I began to believe we were witnessing a miracle. After all, it is extremely difficult for an alcoholic to stop drinking even when he or she is in a sobriety program.

Unfortunately, his years of alcohol abuse had taken their toll on his body, and he was in poor health. Within two years of signing the pledge, he died. On the day that I typed it out, I doubted that he would keep his word; I just wanted to get rid of him. Shame on me. It became clear to me later, though, that he took the pledge seriously. He had mustered the courage to make his vow, then asked God for forgiveness. To my surprise, he was sober to the day he died.

Thereafter, I often thought of him—dirty, disheveled, unable to keep a job, and plagued with an addiction that ruined his life. But in the end, he changed and was forgiven by a merciful God who sees all of us as broken in our own way and is willing to step in to heal us if we but open the door to His love. Miracles do happen.

26. A Christmas Memory

When I was growing up in Williamsport, my father always took me to a barbershop on Market Street for my Christmas haircut. Jim DeSanto and Ed Badman were the barbers who did the pruning. Dad would reward me for sitting still with money to buy Christmas presents for others.

One December day when I was five years old, I waltzed in with my father and took a seat on the wooden pony. I was hoping mightily that Mr. DeSanto would pass me up for another victim. The problem was that whenever he closed the hand clippers on a lock of hair, he would pull them back before they snipped off the lock. It was a form of scalping. Ed Badman, on the other hand, used electric clippers that buzzed off the hair painlessly. All the while, he nurtured my fantasy that I was riding the wooden pony in the Kentucky Derby.

I was in luck. Mr. Badman was my barber on that day. After I won the derby, my father gave me my money—a whole $5—and let me shop just down the street at Lenny's Army and Navy Store. Dad told me that Christmas wasn't just for receiving; it was also for giving.

The owner of Lenny's was a friend of the family. The store was a wonderland of military paraphernalia: pup tents, knapsacks, canteens, camouflage uniforms, hatchets, boots, binoculars. Lenny's also stocked regular clothing and accessories for both men and women.

It wasn't long before I spotted an ideal gift for my father: a beautiful, extra-wide necktie with a hand-painted picture of a horse's head. The clerk, a nice lady, said it cost only $2 and she would wrap it for free.

"I'll take it," I said.

Next, I browsed for a gift for my mother. The lady showed me scarves—some frilly, some woolly—flannel nightgowns, rain hats, umbrellas, wallets, and coin purses.

"Well, I don't know," I said.

Just then I turned around and beheld an item any mother would die for: a Swiss Army knife. It had two blades, which my mother could use to peel potatoes. It also had a corkscrew, a bottle opener, a can opener, and a nail file. Everything folded up into the handle, which would fit nicely in a kitchen drawer. The price was $2.75, and again the wrap job was free.

After I paid for both gifts, I walked out with the presents in a bag and a quarter in change. Not bad.

On Christmas morning, I tore open my gifts: a jack-in-the-box, a spinning top, Lincoln Logs, a yo-yo, and sundry other marvels. Then I presented my gifts to my mother and father. Mom was overwhelmed with joy at the sight of the Swiss Army knife. Later that day, she called me into the kitchen to show me how well the knife could peel potatoes and open cans. After my father opened his gift, he placed the tie around his neck, made a Windsor knot, and said it was the most beautiful thing he had ever seen. He wore it to the 11 o'clock Mass that morning. When he was taking up the collection, you could see the horse's head all the way from the back of the church. How proud he was to wear that tie! The people in the pews craned their necks to see it.

Mom and Dad kept their special gifts for years and now and then would take them out to admire them. Years later, I realized what a beautiful lesson my parents had taught me: It was not the gift that mattered most; it was the love with which it was given—and received.

27. A Tonsil Tale

When I was a child, frequent infections of my tonsils necessitated their removal at Divine Providence Hospital in Williamsport. In those days—the early 1950s—many doctors recommended that brothers or sisters of a patient also have their tonsils removed to prevent infections like mine or other tonsil-related problems. Consequently, when I had my tonsils removed, so did my younger brother, Jim.

The surgical procedure (called a tonsillectomy) remains commonplace today, although it is performed less frequently than in the fifties.

Jim and I waited in a special family room with our parents. When the time for surgery arrived, we were walked to the operating room one at a time. I vividly remember the antiseptic smells, the table with the big light, and the uniformed attendants wearing masks. It was all very intimidating. But then I noticed that one of the masked persons was a nun wearing a white habit instead of the usual dark one. If Sister was there in the operating room, I thought, everything would be okay.

Attendants lifted me onto the operating table and then the anesthetist administered the ether, telling me to breathe deeply. I inhaled and conked out. In what seemed like only a moment later, I woke up in a recovery room. In the bed next to mine was my brother. Both of us had sore throats. The one saving feature was that they gave us ice cream, mound upon mound of it, apparently to relieve the soreness.

After Mom and Dad went home that evening, Jim and I nodded off. A dim louvered light kept watch over us through the night. The next morning, Jim and I received a breakfast that included a bowl of warm oatmeal. Neither of us had had it before, and neither of us liked it when we tasted it. So we let the blobs sit there.

"You can't go home until you eat that," a nurse said after coming in to observe our progress.

Jim cried in the belief that we would be prisoners in that room for the rest of our lives.

"Don't worry," I said after the nurse left. "I have a plan."

Then I took both bowls into the bathroom, dumped the oatmeal into the toilet, and flushed it into oblivion. You might say I performed an oatmeal-ectomy. When I returned, I told Jim not to say a word about my little deception.

When the nurse came back in, I said, "All gone." She was so proud of us.

To this day, I don't like oatmeal. It makes me think of surgery and sore throats.

28. The Shout

Another eventful Sunday at St. Patrick's Church in Wilkes-Barre, I had to contend with terrible acoustics. The large dome and the hard walls converted racing words into resounding babble. So I had to speak slowly and distinctly when I preached.

At the 7am Mass about two minutes into my homily, a young man seated on one side of the church began to snore like a bear in hibernation. His snores circled the dome, then bounced from wall to wall like ping-pong balls. A woman seated next to him—I assume it was his mother—let him have it with her elbow. Surprised and bewildered, he sat straight up and howled from the top of his lungs—Aaaagh!—as if waking from a nightmare.

Everyone laughed. It was a really funny moment. Realizing I could not regain the attention of the parishioners, I hurriedly ended the talk. I'll bet that young man got a talkin' to when he got home. Then again, maybe he received praise, for Psalm 47:2 says, "Acclaim your God with cries of rejoicing."

Ascension Church Williamsport Pa. Easter Sunday 2007

29. Lost and Found

After receiving a new assignment, priests naturally want to make a good impression on the parishioners. It was that way with me when I said my first 11 a.m. Mass at St. Patrick's Church in Wilkes-Barre. I didn't know anyone in the pews, and I felt a little inadequate.

At the offertory, an altar boy brought the chalice to the altar as usual, and I positioned it near the paten, a circular metal plate. In the center of the paten was a large host (wafer of unleavened bread). As is customary, I raised the paten slightly above the surface of the altar, using both hands, while saying the offertory prayer over the host. Next, I set the paten on the corporal, a white linen cloth, then stepped to the side of the altar with the chalice to receive a small amount of wine and a trickle of water from cruets held by the altar boys.

When I returned to the center of the altar, I was astonished to see that the host was no longer on the paten. After searching for it on the surface of the altar, I stepped back and checked the floor around the altar. The host was nowhere to be seen. Then I thought that it might have fallen into a fold of my chasuble, the sleeveless outer garment that a priest wears during Mass. So I began to shake and flap it, hoping that the host would come loose.

During this interlude, the congregation was observing their new assistant pastor in the process of losing his mind. I suppose I looked like an injured bird flapping wildly to leave the ground. Meanwhile, one of the altar boys spotted the host. It had rolled into a cranny beneath the altar. While he got down on his belly to attempt to retrieve it, I sent the other altar boy to the sacristy to get another host. I then explained to the congregation that a flap of my chasuble had brushed the missing host off the paten and into its hiding place. Fortunately, the lost host had not yet been consecrated, so it was still unleavened bread.

When the boy on the floor got up with the lost host, the other came in with another host. There was laughter.

Whenever a funny happenstance interrupts Mass, the best response for a priest is to acknowledge what happened, share the laughter of the moment, then put on a serious face and resume the liturgy. God excuses our clumsiness—and probably chuckles at it.

30. The Balloon

As I began Mass one day, a balloon started floating around the church. When an incoming parishioner opened the east door, a blast of air blew the balloon across the church. When the back door opened, the balloon wafted toward the altar.

I was saying the Saturday vigil Mass at St. Paul's Church in Scranton for Msgr. John O'Brien. Earlier in the day, there had been a wedding at which the bride's friends and family decorated the church with balloons. Thank God that practice has gone out of vogue.

Anyway, the balloon at the vigil Mass continued to float during Mass. The eyes of children and many adults followed the balloon instead of the celebration of Mass. Perhaps in the sermon I should have compared the balloon to the transgressor who blows with the prevailing winds, or to a temptation that blows us from the righteous path.

In the procession to the back of the church at the end of Mass, the cross bearer led the way down the middle aisle, followed by two acolytes with candles and the lector with the book. Just as I stepped into the middle aisle from the sanctuary to join the procession, the balloon descended toward me. I reached up, grabbed the string attached to it, and fished it in. Beautiful hand-eye coordination, I thought. Then when I placed the balloon under my arm, it popped.

After Mass a woman approached me and asked, very seriously, "Father, did you plan that, the capturing of the balloon?" How do you answer a question like that? What would your answer be?

31. Preaching

After serving ten years in the hospital ministry in the Scranton Diocese, I was to be assigned to parish work again. The year was 1994. Because I did not want to become a pastor immediately, Bishop James C. Timlin assigned me to serve as the senior priest at a very busy church, St. Jude's in Mountain Top. This assignment would allow me to readapt to parish work without the responsibility of being pastor. I was 52 at the time.

Father Paul Mullen was the pastor of St. Jude's, and Father Joe Evanko was his assistant. Before I arrived, I was aware of their reputation as two of the best speakers in the diocese. Fr. Mullen, who had years of experience in parish ministry, could weave a beautiful story and lesson out of the most insignificant topic. He was a great storyteller.

Fr. Evanko, a young priest just a few years out of the seminary who identified with the young couples and children of the parish, was a master at using visual aids to enliven his homilies. He was so good that he was asked to teach homiletics to the diaconate candidates in the diocese.

So there I was, an older priest serving with two younger priests who were expert preachers. At the hospital, I was used to giving homilies to busy hospital employees who often had to hurry back to work. Consequently, many of my homilies were brief and superficial. Because I felt intimidated in my new assignment, I preferred saying Masses at our two mission churches to avoid being compared with these two giants, as I perceived them.

However, I later decided I had the wrong attitude toward preaching. The right approach was to prepare and deliver a straightforward sermon—without trying to entertain the congregation—then have faith that the Holy Spirit would move the listeners to absorb what they heard and act on it in their daily lives.

One Sunday after Mass, a woman came up to me and said she felt that St. Jude had the three best preachers in the diocese. Wow! I needed that vote of confidence. Then she said, "You are different."

That was true. We prepared differently, we used different techniques, and we approached scriptures in a different way. However, each of us was effective in his own way; each of us had his own God-given talent to proclaim the Word and allow the Holy Spirit to move the people. "[It is] not I, but Christ who lives in me" (Galatians 2:20).

32. Why Were They Laughing?

At Mass one Sunday in a tent at Effort, Pa., I made a fool of myself while preaching the homily.

Among the attendees were Scouts from a nearby camp. How gentlemanly they were, I thought, when I noticed that they waited for all the parishioners to seat themselves on folding chairs before they sat down themselves. The Scout leaders had taught them well.

My homily that day centered on St. Stephen. As you may recall, he was recruited by the Apostles to preach the message of Christianity in Jerusalem. When he did so, certain members of his audience rejected his message and, they hired henchmen to accuse him of blasphemy. Later, a mob stoned him to death, making him Christianity's first martyr.

During the homily, the Scouts broke out into a round of sniggers, then loud guffaws. I paused for a moment as I wondered what they were laughing at. When I resumed the sermon at the place where I left off, they laughed again. All I did was say, "St. Stephen was stoned."

After Mass, I told the assistant pastor, Fr. Galligan, about the incident. In response, he asked me the subject of my sermon. I told him, repeating phrases I had used. Then, chuckling, he explained my gaffe.

From that time on, I became very careful with every word in my homilies, paying attention to what Mark Twain wrote in a letter to a friend in 1888:

"The difference between the almost right word and the right word is really a large matter—it's the difference between the lightning bug and the lightning."

33. Saints I Met

Saint John Paul II

I met Pope John Paul II in 1982 while participating in a three-month study program at the pastoral institute of the North American College in Rome, Italy. The program included a private audience in the Vatican with His Holiness. At 8:30 a.m. on the appointed day, Swiss Guards escorted our group to the papal apartments to meet with the Pope in one of several halls he used for morning audiences with four or five groups.

We sat on chairs arranged in rows before a platform with a large chair for the Pope. Moments later, he arrived with staff members and seated himself on the platform. After he spoke to us for a few minutes, we lined up to meet with him one at a time. He asked each of us, "Is your mother still living?" When my turn came, I told him my mother was indeed alive. Then he said, "Give this to your mother." The gift was a beautiful white rosary in a small brown packet. Years before, my mother had received the gift of a crystal rosary from her pastor, Msgr. Frank P. McHugh. However, she lost it. To receive the white rosary from the Pope to replace the crystal rosary was a special surprise.

Saint Theresa of Calcutta

When I was director of the Society for the Propagation of the Faith of the Diocese of Scranton, Mother Theresa came to Scranton to give a talk to all the sisters working in the diocese. While in the city, she visited the diocesan chancery office to meet with Bishop J. Carroll McCormick. All chancery employees assembled in the hallway to greet Mother Theresa collectively and individually. As director of the missions, my visit with her was especially important since her sisters were interested in coming to Scranton to appeal for donations at parishes. She was very pleasant but extremely focused on her mission. No personal banter was exchanged.

Venerable Walter Ciszak

After serving twenty-five years at hard labor in a Soviet prison camp, Fr. Walter Ciszak gained his release and later wrote the book *With God in Russia*, which became a bestseller. His sister was a member of the Bernadine Sisters, who maintain a retreat house in Mt. Pocono. It was there that I met Fr. Ciszak. The many years he spent in the bleakness of a gulag did not embitter him, for he was a joyful man with a ready smile who was more than willing to discuss his prison life. He dined with me and other priests at St. Mary's in Mt. Pocono on several occasions and was delightful company.

Father Patrick Peyton

I met Fr. Patrick Peyton briefly in the hallway of the chancery office of the Diocese of Scranton after he visited Bishop J. Carroll McCormick. Fr. Peyton lived in Scranton after he and members of his family came to this country from Ireland during the Great Depression. Jobs were scarce, but Patrick Peyton was hired as a janitor at St. Peter's Cathedral in Scranton. While working at the church, he decided to become a priest. Because of Peyton's advanced age, Bishop Thomas Charles O'Reilly suggested that he join a religious community. Peyton chose the Holy Cross Fathers at Notre Dame in South Bend, Ind. He is most famous for his Rosary Crusades in the 1940's and 50's. His rallying cry was "The family that prays together stays together." His cause for canonization is now under consideration.

Venerable Fulton J. Sheen

Bishop Fulton J. Sheen visited Marywood College in Scranton one summer to give a retreat for priests. I was not making the retreat, but I attended his talks at Marywood. What a great speaker! He was superb even though he was addressing a small group of priests. After the talks and at lunch one afternoon, I was able to talk with Bishop Sheen. My connection was my role as diocesan director of the Propagation of the Faith. Bishop Sheen had been this organization's national director for twenty-five years. We spoke of the missions, and he expressed interest in the missionaries from the Scranton Diocese. He was acquainted with many of our missionaries and commended them for their work in the mission fields.

34. Lessons in Forgiveness and Humility

Baseball was America's most popular sport when I was growing up. Every kid in every town learned the game, hoping to follow in the footsteps of Joe DiMaggio or Stan Musial. I was no exception.

At the time—the 1940s and early fifties—I was living with my parents in the Kelly Apartments on Campbell Street in Williamsport. The building was a grand edifice with a stained glass window over the ornate front door.

In the spacious backyard of this dwelling, I learned to play baseball under the tutelage of two neighbor boys, Bud and Duck Welshans. They were older than I was, but they graciously allowed me to play catch with them. My father would also sometimes play catch with me or hit grounders for me to scoop up like Yankee shortstop Phil Rizzuto.

At age nine, I was good enough to make a team in the Maynard Little League, about a half-mile away. On my first at bat, the pitcher had trouble finding the strike zone because I was so short. So I drew a walk. Rarin' to go, I stole second the next time the pitcher threw the ball. What an easy game, I thought, dusting myself off. On the following pitch, I stole third. By this time, I realized I was a David against nine Goliaths. They couldn't stop me. So, when the next batter stepped in and the pitcher released the ball, I took off for home plate. But before I got halfway down the base path, the catcher was already standing erect with the baseball. He could have had tea and crumpets while waiting for me. After he tagged me out, I slouched to the dugout, my head hanging low, while the opposing players spat choice words in my direction.

The Bible says, "Everyone who exalts himself shall be humbled" (Luke 14:11).

Those words were taught in every Catholic school, including mine. Nevertheless, as my arm grew stronger and my throw more accurate, I began to fancy myself as the new Cy Young or Walter Johnson. I took to practicing in front of the house, throwing the ball against the steps. Day after day, I threw the ball—harder and harder. I got so good I began to put on throwing demonstrations just in case anyone across the street was observing.

During one demonstration, I threw a raging fastball so far off the mark that it sailed right through that stained glass over the front door. My mother ran out of the house to see if I had been hurt. After I assured her I was all right, she said, "Wait till your father gets home!"

Head hanging, I went inside and found my ego on the floor, shattered into a million pieces of stained glass. Curses, humbled again.

Fortunately for me, the owner of the house—Judge Charles Williams—understood that I had no malice aforethought. When I stood before him in his chambers, believing I was destined for jail, he said, "Charles, did you get hurt?" When I answered no, he replied, "That's good, because we can fix the window, but we cannot always fix you. Don't worry. We will get the window fixed and everything will be okay."

His kind and forgiving manner so impressed me that over the years—including my nearly fifty years in the priesthood—I have always used his approach when dealing with people. And, oh yes, I have also learned not to exalt myself—or at least I try not to—lest the devil be waiting to tag me out.

35. The Sinner in the Last Pew

"Two men went up into the temple to pray; one was a Pharisee, the other a publican (tax collector). The Pharisee stood upright, and made this prayer in his heart, I thank you, God, that I am not like the rest of men, who steal and cheat and commit adultery, or like this publican here; for myself, I fast twice in the week, I give tithes of all that I possess. And the publican stood far off; he would not even lift up his eyes towards heaven; he only beat his breast, and said, God, be merciful to me; I am a sinner. I tell you, this man went back home higher in God's favor than the other; everyone who exalts himself shall be humbled, and the man who humbles himself shall be exalted" (Luke 18:10-14).

Every priest knows parishioners like the Pharisee and the tax collector.

I remember a man in his late seventies who never married, had no family, and lived alone in a modest apartment. Whatever money he earned from menial labor he spent on gambling and drinking. To the best of my knowledge, he never bothered anyone, never became unruly or abusive, and never got into trouble with the law. He was always polite and always clean and shaven. However, guilt plagued him because he could not overcome his gambling and drinking habits no matter how hard he tried.

Every morning for more than thirty years, he attended any church that was open for an early Mass and sat in the back with his head bowed for ten minutes before Mass. During Mass, he would usually receive communion. Afterward, he remained in church for ten more minutes, kneeling with his head bowed. He was probably saying the tax collector's prayer, "O God, be merciful to me, a sinner."

One Sunday as I was greeting parishioners in the back of the church after Mass, I overheard one person say to another, "Who does he think he is coming to church? He's nothing but a drunk and a gambler." Unwittingly, that person was paraphrasing the words of the Pharisee.

Which parishioner do you think, in the words quoted from St. Luke's Gospel, "went back home higher in God's favor than the other"?

I can tell you this. That poor man in the back of the church never knew how much his quiet piety influenced my prayer life. I figured that if this man, who regarded himself as a terrible sinner, could spend more than an hour in church every day, I should spend more time in prayer and contrition pleading my own case. Again, in the words of the tax collector, "O God, be merciful to me, a sinner."

36. **A Penitent Child**

Hearing children's confessions is such a beautiful experience. Whenever I administer the Sacrament of Reconciliation to little ones before Christmas or Easter, or before their first Holy Communion, I marvel at their innocence.

One day when I was hearing confessions in a room at a Catholic school, a little boy recited the usual children's sins: disobedience, lying, being mean to brothers and sisters, etc. After he finished and I gave him absolution, he got up, crossed the room, then walked back toward me and said, "Father, I will really try to do better." This little boy inspired me. If he was willing to try to do better, shouldn't I try to do better as well? I thank God for the inspiring words of an eight-year-old who innocently wants to do better and please his Lord.

37. A Child's Advice

One summer day while assisting in one of our churches in the Poconos, I put on vestments which were very heavy for the time of year. It was in the mid-1970s, before many churches in the diocese—including this one—had installed air-conditioning.

However, it was not my place to complain about vestments or to question how Masses were celebrated. It was my job to do whatever was asked of me. On this particular day, the temperature was about 95 degrees.

At the end of Mass while standing at the door to greet people leaving the church, I was really uncomfortable. Perspiration was pouring from my face. A little boy about four years old came up to me, observed my discomfort, and said, "Why are you wearing that heavy blanket?" He was referring to my chasuble, the outer garment a priest wears during Mass. I answered, "That is a very good question." Then I immediately removed the chasuble. Instant relief!

Since that time, I have never worn a chasuble in a very hot church. I always explain why to the people, telling them that a little boy had the good sense years ago to question why I was "wearing a blanket" on a very hot day.

38. A Child's Enthusiasm

You can't see heaven, but you can see reflections of it in the serene joy of children about to receive their first Holy Communion. Dressed all in white, hands pressed prayerfully together, they approach the altar with a profound bliss that seems otherworldly.

I remember a little girl who was an inspiration to me and other adults at a parish where I once served. Each Sunday, she would get in line with other communicants, assume an attitude of reverence and, with deep felicity in her eyes, move forward. But when she reached the front of the line, she would turn around and return to her seat.

The following week—and several weeks thereafter—she did the same. One Sunday morning after Mass as I was greeting parishioners, I stopped the little girl as she was leaving and asked her how old she was.

"I am eight years old and in the second grade," she said.

"Oh, so you will be receiving your first Holy Communion in May?"

"Yes, Father, and I just can't wait."

Over the next several weeks, she continued to approach the altar, peeking out from one side to watch my movements and to observe her mother's reception of the sacrament. Then, of course, she would return to her seat after reaching the front of the line.

If only all of us could have the spirit of anticipation and prayerfulness of this little girl. So excited was she about the day when she herself would receive Christ that she couldn't contain her enthusiasm by remaining in her pew. She had to take her place in line to get a feel for the experience.

That little girl, by her actions, inspired me to be more attentive and prayerful at communion time and more thankful for the gift of the Body and Blood of Jesus in the Holy Eucharist. We must never let the reception of the Eucharist become routine and unremarkable.

39. The Sounds of Piety

In the early seventies, four priests served the people of St. Mary's Church in Dunmore. I was one of them. Each of us celebrated Mass every weekday morning, one at 6am and the other three at 7, 7:30, and 8am. Yet one parishioner spent more time in church than we did. He was in his eighties and lived alone just down the street from the church. I will call him Mr. Anthony (which was not his real name).

Mr. Anthony attended all the morning Masses and sometimes remained in his pew until noon. In the afternoon, he often returned to church to pray the rosary.

His piety was praiseworthy, even heroic. All the other parishioners loved him for the example he set for them and their children. Unfortunately, when saying a prayer or praying the rosary, he hissed and whistled like a steam locomotive; now and then he chirped like a newly hatched chick. When Mass began, he stopped his private praying and started shouting the responses. When the congregation chanted or sang a song, he was always one or two beats ahead of everyone else—and very loud.

Respectfully, we pleaded, begged, and beseeched him to lower his voice and muffle his sounds when praying and to chant and sing in unison with the others. But nothing changed.

Families would ask us not to tell Mr. Anthony about weddings or funerals they were arranging, for he would surely be there praying aloud if he knew about them.

After Mr. Anthony died in his sleep one night, a pall of heavy silence fell over the church during services. We missed Mr. Anthony. He had reminded us of the importance of prayer in our daily lives. The church was full for his funeral. However, truth be told, we did not miss the loudness of his piety. There was no hissing or whistling, no chirping. He was at peace, and so were we.

I wonder, though, whether in some corner of heaven can be heard the sound of—well, never mind. If making a little noise was his only fault, let us rejoice and be glad.

40. The Compassion of Nurses

In my fifteen years of hospital ministry, I marveled time and again at the bravery, skill, and compassion of nurses. Nursing is a noble but difficult and demanding profession, requiring special dedication to patients and their needs.

One day, when I entered the room of a woman dying slowly of the infirmities of old age, I saw a nurse sitting alongside her stroking her hand. The woman's mind was impaired and she was nearing the end.

As I walked toward the bed, the nurse began reciting the Twenty-Third Psalm.

"The Lord is my shepherd. I shall not want. In verdant pastures, he gives me repose; beside restful waters he leads me. He restores my soul."

The patient seemed comforted by the serenity and rhythm of the words as the nurse continued.

"You guide me along the right path for your name's sake. Even though I walk through the valley of death, I fear no evil for you are at my side with your rod and staff to give me courage."

The nurse sensed my presence and turned toward me. She explained that the woman had no visitors, for she had no family left. Most of her friends were also deceased. So the nurse had decided to spend all of her break time with the patient. She talked to her and comforted her—and prayed—to ease the poor woman's suffering in her final hours.

I was deeply moved by the kindness and concern of this nurse for the elderly woman. To give up her own rest time to sit with this dying woman was an act of unsolicited love and caring that was profoundly inspiring to witness. But her selfless action was never rewarded by the hospital, for she carried it out so quietly. She did not receive—and did not expect—any special recognition for giving love and repose to her patient.

I saw other nurses perform similar acts of quiet love for their patients—acts that the public never saw or heard about. However, I know that God saw their kindness and will one day reward them for it. For the Lord has said, "Whatever you do for the least of my brothers or sisters, you do it to for me" (Matthew 25:40).

Pastor Ascension and Holy Rosary Churches Williamsport Pa.
(Pastor 1997-2009)

41. **Listen to the Children**

In the 1980s, a religious denomination sponsored a short TV spot focusing on a little girl in a party dress who had just returned home. The ad was so effective in getting its point across that I began repeating its message in sermons.

First, the little girl—about six—runs to the kitchen, where her mother is preparing dinner for the family.

"Mommy, Mommy," she says excitedly. "It was a wonderful party. We played games and had cake and—"

"Oh, not now, honey," the mother says, "I'm busy getting supper ready. Go tell your father about it."

The girl runs out to the garage, where her father is covered in grease and grime as he works on the family car.

"Daddy, I want to tell you about the wonderful party I went to. We had so much fun playing games and—"

"Not now," he says. "I've got to get this car fixed, and you'd get yourself dirty walking around in here. Go tell your sister."

The little girl then runs to a bedroom, where her older sister is putting on makeup while getting ready for a big date.

"Sis, let me tell you about the party. Mary and Janie were there and we had cake and—"

"Not now," the sister says. "I'm going out. Tell me about it tomorrow."

Sadly, the little girl goes out to the back porch and sits on the top step. The family's golden retriever comes from the yard and sits next to her. When she puts her arm around the dog, it sits quietly, licks her hand, and listens while the little girl talks.

"I just came back from a wonderful party. We had chocolate cake and played games. Mary and Janie and all my friends were there. I had the greatest time."

Once again the dog licks her face. A voice-over can be heard saying, "Don't let your children go to the dogs." The mother, father, and sister didn't intend to be unkind or insensitive to the little girl; they were just "too busy" to listen to her at a particular moment.

What a powerful visual lesson and great story for a homily.

42. A Parishioner's Strange Behavior

My father was a good source of stories that I have used in homilies over the years. One of his stories was about an elderly woman named Maggie who belonged to the same Williamsport church he attended, Annunciation.

Maggie first came to his attention when he was a boy attending Sunday Mass in the early 1920s. As the priest and altar servers walked up the middle aisle at the beginning of Mass, Maggie left her pew and joined the procession. In fact, she led it.

"What was really odd," my father said, "was that she was carrying a stack of newspapers."

When she reached the sanctuary, she placed the stack of newspapers on the altar railing and returned to her seat. (Until the early 1970s, marble or wooden railings supported by posts divided the sanctuary of Catholic churches from the seating area.) Shortly before the distribution of Holy Communion, she walked up the middle aisle again and retrieved the stack. No one ever learned from her the significance of her newspaper ritual, which she repeated at Mass many times thereafter. Perhaps she was hoping that the prayers said at Mass would lead to a day when there were only positive stories in the news—no war, no crime, and so on.

On the occasions when a priest would walk up and down the aisles to sprinkle holy water on the congregation, Maggie would attract attention in another way. Just before the priest reached her pew, she would open an umbrella to avoid getting wet.

Maggie also exhibited other forms of strange behavior—like trying to balance her pocketbook on the ridge running across the top of a pew. After it teetered and tottered, she would usually get it to balance precariously. It may be that she was hoping for heavenly intervention to balance her budget.

Whatever the case, Maggie taught the congregation that the Lord welcomes all kinds of people into His house. It is our duty to make them feel at home even though are "different" in some way.

43. An Inspiring Story From Bishop Sheen

Between 1952 and 1957, Bishop Fulton J. Sheen hosted a TV show in which he discussed important moral issues. It was among the highest-rated programs of its day. After Sheen won an Emmy, comedian Milton Berle, who had his own show in the same time slot, said, "He's got better writers—Matthew, Mark, Luke, and John." Our family rarely missed Bishop Sheen's show, called *Life Is Worth Living*.

One memorable story he told was about his trip to the mission country in Africa, where he visited many churches in remote areas and said Mass. At Holy Communion time on one occasion, he was shocked when he saw a man approaching the altar on his hands and knees. After the bishop gave him communion, he watched the man crawl to the back of the church.

"Why does he do that?" Bishop Sheen later asked the pastor.

The pastor explained that the man suffered from leprosy. Some of his fingers and toes had fallen off. Others were barely hanging on. Unable to walk, he crawled wherever he had to go. Every day, he crawled half-a-mile to Mass and another half-mile when he returned home. The pastor said he offered to take communion to the man at his home, but the man insisted on attending church. His crawling was a both a sacrifice for Jesus and a form of penance for his sins.

Bishop Sheen's topic on the show in which he told this story focused on sacrifice and mortification. All of us, he said, are called upon to make sacrifices and do penance ourselves. The African man did not shirk his duty. Moreover, he was not bitter or angry about his affliction.

Some of us find it a challenge to spend five or ten minutes a day praying on our knees. This man spent many hours each day on his hands and knees to expiate his sins and please God.

One can only marvel at such a man and hope that his example continues to live in the memories of all of us.

44. Life After Life

It was a privilege for me to serve for fifteen years as a chaplain at two hospitals, a job that I enjoyed immensely. During that time, I received the usual requests to pray for patients or administer the Sacrament of the Sick. But sometimes I also received requests for miracles. On such occasions, I simply encouraged relatives and friends of patients—or the patients themselves—to pray for a recovery or, in the case of the terminally ill, a happy death. A miracle was an extremely rare event, I told them. Only God could provide one.

One day, I was called to the intensive care unit to see a woman who had suffered a cardiac arrest a few hours before. (A cardiac arrest is a malfunction of the heart that results in death within minutes unless the patient receives CPR. It is not the same as a heart attack.) Though tired and scared, the woman seemed to be of sound mind and was able to talk lucidly about her experience. But it was not her resuscitation that she talked about. It was what happened to her after slipped into unconsciousness. She said she was lifted out of her body to a point over her bed. There, she observed nurses and a doctor working on her. She felt calm; a strange light shone around her bed as work on her continued.

I was skeptical. From my experience, I well knew that many medications can cause bizarre, vivid dreams. However, she was adamant that what she experienced was not a dream. She insisted that she had witnessed what really happened—as it was happening.

I asked, "Who was the doctor who worked on you?"

She identified the physician by name. I checked the name against the roster of ER doctors working that day. It was on the list. Moreover, records showed that this doctor was the one who worked on her. She could not have been told the doctor's identity, for neither the doctor nor the nurses had yet spoken with her about her close call.

As to what she saw during her episode, I was the first person in the hospital to hear of it. She had confided in me, she said, because she thought I was the one person who might believe her. I *did* believe her. My previous check of hospital records—and my subsequent conversations with the nurses in the ICU—convinced me of the truthfulness of her story. Apparently, this woman had undergone what was commonly referred to as an out-of-body experience. She was on the threshold between life and death, but was pulled back from it.

It may be that on certain rare occasions, God enables some of us to take one step over that threshold, then step back again to report our encounter with the supernatural to bolster the faith of those struggling with doubt. But even when doubt persists in such people, they can look to the Bible to strengthen their faith—to the story of Lazarus of Bethany, whom Jesus restored to life four days after his death (John 11) and to the resurrection of Christ himself, as testified to by all four Gospel writers.

We don't know exactly what will happen when the time comes for us to cross the threshold. But if we are truly penitent, Jesus will be there for us. So we must be prepared to meet Him and, in the meantime, ask the Blessed Virgin to—in the words of the Hail Mary— "Pray for us sinners, now, and at the hour of our death."

45. Why Did You Revive Me?

I got to know Mr. Michaels very well during his stay in the hospital. He was in his late eighties. His family had all died, and he had few friends left to visit him.

On my daily visits to his room, he told me about his life as a coal miner and his struggle to feed his family on the meager wages miners received in the 1930s and 1940s. Remarkably, though, he and his wife were able to make enough sacrifices to put their five children through college. By the time he retired in 1959, he had developed miner's asthma, also called black lung disease. Because it reduced his ability to move around freely, he spent most of his days at home. His wife was a loving woman who helped and cared for him until she died unexpectedly one day. After he was admitted to the hospital, his children, who lived in other parts of the country, came to see him when they could.

It was interesting to talk with Mr. Michaels about the mines—especially about how he managed to cope in dark and dusty tunnels underground when, at any moment, earth and rocks could come crashing down on him. He told me he was in the mines on January 22, 1959, the day that the Susquehanna River came thundering down into the whole mine system in the Scranton and Wilkes-Barre area, killing twelve men. Other miners managed to make it to high ground before the raging waters could swallow them up. The disaster ended the mining industry in one frightful instant. However, Mr. Michaels was old enough to be able to retire with a pension.

One day during his stay in the hospital, he stopped breathing. When his monitors transmitted an alarm, hospital staff members rushed to his room and were able to revive him. When he awoke, he grabbed the arm of the first nurse he saw and said, "Why did you bring me back?"

His question unnerved the staff members, especially the nurse he grabbed. Had they done something wrong? What did his question mean? Here is what they concluded: Mr. Michaels wanted to die because he was old, his wife was gone, his children lived elsewhere, and he felt useless.

When I next visited him, he told me his version of the story. After he lapsed into unconsciousness, he beheld a beautiful light that he could feel as well as see, he said. The light enveloped him with calmness and love; he could feel a comforting presence. He was hesitant to say that this presence was God, but he felt so at peace that he did not want to leave that presence. In a moment, though, he awoke to his hospital setting, with five nurses and a physician standing around him. He was back in the world of pain and suffering.

After he was stabilized, he rested for a while. Then he asked to speak with the nurse whose arm he grabbed.

"I'm sorry I scared you," he told her. Then he explained what happened to him. Later, he told me about the experience and asked, "Father, do you think that I was in the presence of God?" I did not answer his question with an emphatic yes. But I did believe he was in the presence of God and that everything he saw while being worked on happened just as he described it.

46. Keeping My Precious Thumbs

During my summer vacation from college in 1961, I worked for Radiant Steel Company in Williamsport in a good-paying job that helped defray the cost of my education. Among the company's most important products were steel covers for radiators and steel boxes for furnaces.

Giant machines formed flat sheets of steel into the required shapes, punched out louvers for ventilation, and made small assembly parts from pieces of steel.

My job was to assist mechanics who set up and serviced the machines and adjusted their working parts to precise measurements. While they worked on the machines, I handed them tools, ran errands, and moved piles of steel to the machines on carts. I was a gofer.

One day, the boss assigned me a simple task at one of the big machines: to place 1x3-inch flats of steel into a machine one at a time, then press a pedal that lowered the machine onto the flat to form an L-shaped hook. These hooks were used in the installation of the covers and boxes.

"One at a time," the boss told me. "One at a time. You got it?"

Next to me was a barrel full of the flats of steel to be crushed into hooks. One at a time, I placed them into the machine, pressed the pedal, and made hooks. I continued doing this for the rest of my shift. The next day, I resumed making the hooks one at a time. The task was boring and tedious. After an hour, I began making two at a time. After another hour, I made four at a time by holding the small pieces in place with my thumbs while pressing the pedal. I was making good progress until my foot slipped as the machine was coming down. I lost my balance, the four steel flats went flying, and my thumbs ended up under the machine. Fortunately, a safety device was triggered when my foot slipped. The machine stopped just one inch above my thumbs.

The boss saw what had happened and, after noticing that I was not hurt, let me have it with both barrels.

"You nitwit, if those thumbs had come off I would have been the one they would have blamed."

He was right. I was told to make the hooks one at a time, but I didn't follow orders. I was wrong and nearly lost my thumbs because of it.

If I had lost my thumbs, I would have been disqualified as a candidate for the priesthood. In those days, the church did not allow anyone with such a physical impediment to become a priest. The rules have changed since then so that special dispensations can be granted for handicaps.

47. The Mourner

An elderly man in the parish where I was serving lived alone and received few, if any, visitors because he had outlived most of his friends and family. After he died, the Altar and Rosary Society recited the rosary at his viewing, but only two or three others attended to pay their respects.

The next day, only a few parishioners showed up for the funeral. However, there was one man in the congregation who appeared deeply upset. Perhaps he was close to the deceased—or so everyone thought.

At the cemetery, a parishioner asked, "Were you a close friend of this man?"

"No," he said. "But he was my brother."

Listeners appeared puzzled. Then he explained: "We haven't spoken to each other for over fifty years."

"That's too bad," the priest said. "What happened?"

"We had a fight and never again spoke to each other. I feel so bad about that."

"What did you fight about?" the priest said.

"I don't remember," the brother replied.

It's so sad when family members fight and argue, then become so angry that they refuse to speak to each other. Of course, we cannot judge these brothers too harshly. After all, we don't know whether one or the other tried to reconcile over the years but was rebuffed. Clearly, though, their argument years before had led to the destruction of their relationship.

The apostle Peter once asked Jesus, "Lord, how often must I see my brother do me wrong, and still forgive him; as much as seven times?" Jesus replied, "I tell you to forgive, not seven wrongs, but seventy times seven." (Matthew 18: 21-22).

Forgiveness is a virtue that sets Christianity apart from many other religions. We Catholics pray every day in the Our Father, "Forgive us our trespasses as we forgive those who trespass against us." Let us take these words to heart.

48. Mass on a Stage

After being assigned as a summer assistant pastor at St. Ann's Parish in Tobyhanna in 1968, I had to say Mass one Sunday on a stage in one of our churches. It was a moving experience. But let me acquaint you first with the parish.

St. Ann's served an extensive territory that included four other churches: Our Lady of the Lake, Pocono Pines; St. Rita's, Gouldsboro; St. Mary Magdalene, South Sterling; and St. Anthony's, Newfoundland. So I would be going places.

That first Sunday Mass was at St. Anthony's, which was a theater-in-the-round. On the stage were chairs for the celebrant and two servers, an altar, and a lectern. After I put on my vestments in a dressing room that doubled as a sacristy, the servers and I walked over a bridge to the altar.

As I began Mass, I realized that only the dim lights were on, so I asked an altar boy to get someone to turn on the bright lights. He spoke with a man in the congregation who was the caretaker of the theater/church. The caretaker then went to a control panel and began flipping switches. However, besides turning on the main lights, he also flipped a switch that started a motor. A moment later, the stage began rotating like a slow-moving merry-go-round. There I was trying to say Mass on a stage going round and round. Where and when it would stop, nobody knew. It was indeed a moving experience.

On his way back to his pew, the caretaker saw what was happening and returned to the control panel. Unfortunately, he had trouble finding the motor switch. Meanwhile, the altar kept rotating. The people in the congregation began to laugh, the servers began to laugh, and I began to laugh. The Mass could not continue until he shut off the motor at the precise moment when the stage had returned to its original position.

Two minutes passed. More laughter.

Finally, the caretaker pressed the right switch at the right time. But the laughter continued for two more minutes before I was able to resume Mass.

Every Mass setting, every congregation, and every celebrant are different. Anything can happen. The only unchangeable element—the only thing that remains consistent and eternal—is the mystery of the Eucharist. In this mystery, bread and wine become the body and blood of Jesus Christ. You and I are invited to receive this gift. When we do, we truly *do* have a moving experience if we take the time to realize that we are becoming one with Christ.

49. Echoes in the Confessional

Christmastime at St. Mary's Church in Dunmore meant hours and hours of hearing confessions in old-style confessionals with three compartments. The priest sat in the middle, behind a closed door. In the compartments on the left and right, each penitent knelt before a screen and a sliding panel. The priest slid back the panel on the right to hear the confession of the person behind the screen, then closed it when the confession concluded. He then slid back the panel on the left to hear the confession of the person behind the other screen.

One day, after about two hours of hearing confessions, I slid back the panel on one side and heard two boys saying, "Bless me, father, for I have sinned" (the words recited at the beginning of each confession). However, they spoke one after the other, making it sound as if the second child's words were echoes of the first child's words.

First boy: "It is two weeks since my last confession."
Second boy: "It is two weeks since my last confession."
Me: "How many of you are there?"

A little voice said, "Two of us. I forgot how to go to confession so my friend said he would come in to help me."

I did not react audibly, but inwardly I was roaring with laughter. Quietly, I told the friend to leave, promising to help the other with his confession.

Helping others is a commendable goal to teach young children, but these boys didn't understand that doing it in a confessional was going too far. The late TV host Art Linkletter wrote a book entitled *Kids Say the Darndest Things*. But kids also *do* the darndest things, and to me these two boys did one of the darndest.

50. Sister Mary Richard

My sophomore homeroom teacher at St. Joseph's School in 1958 was Sr. Mary Richard, a member of the IHM religious community (Sisters, Servants of the Immaculate Heart of Mary). My classmates and I all assumed that she was a hundred years old and therefore was unaware of the mischief we were up to.

In April, just before the beginning of our Easter vacation, we sophomore boys decided at lunchtime to start the vacation early by taking the afternoon off to play basketball at a nearby court. Sr. Mary Richard, because of her diminished powers of observation at her advanced age, would never notice our absence. Or so we thought. If any mother found out where we were, we would just say that the whole school got out early for Easter. What we didn't know when we left for the basketball court was that the principal, Mother Willemyn, was going to dismiss classes early anyway.

However, nothing went as planned, and we sophomore boys ended up with the worst possible punishment—the wrath of the rest of the entire student body. Here's what happened. After lunch, Sr. Mary Richard *did* notice our absence and reported it Mother Willemyn. She, in turn, decided that classes would remain in session while telephone calls were made to the mothers of each missing boy.

Meanwhile, after our basketball game, we boys dispersed. I headed toward Smith's Drug Store, which was a block from St. Joe's. I worked there as a clerk on weekdays after school. On my way, I saw my mother steaming toward me like an angry locomotive. Her head was down, in the "I will accept absolutely no excuse" position. I then removed my driver's permit from my wallet and gave it to her, figuring she was going to take it anyway as punishment. She looked at it and said, "Hmpf." Then she spoke the feared words:

"You just wait until your father gets home!"

Later, my father passed sentence: grounding. At school after the vacation, Mother Willemyn passed sentence: detention for all of us truants.

But our punishment didn't end there. The rest of the student body treated us as reprobate bums for weeks afterward for robbing them of an afternoon off.

Sometime later, as I was going to class, I met Sr. Mary Richard in the hallway. Out of the blue, she said to me, "Charles, one day you are going to become a priest." I was stunned. How did she know I was considering the priesthood as my vocation? I had told no one about it, not even my parents. Maybe she was just prodding me to consider that vocation, I thought.

After high school, I did pursue a path toward the priesthood and was ordained in 1968. I didn't see her again until 1986. Aware that I was a chaplain at Mercy Hospital in Scranton, she called me from the Marian Convent across town to ask me to come to see her. She was then one month shy of her 97th birthday. After I entered her room, she said, "Charles, will you celebrate my funeral Mass?"

"Don't be talking like that," I replied.

But she said, "I am going to die soon, and I would like you to say the funeral Mass. Will you do it?"

"Yes, Sister," I said, like an obedient student.

About two weeks later, I was at the chapel of the Marian Convent celebrating her funeral Mass. Here was a woman who had spent nearly seventy-four years in the service of God, the IHM sisters, and thousands of children—from Aug. 2, 1912, the date of her profession of religious vows, to July 3, 1986, the date of her death. This sharp old cookie wasn't the absent-minded teacher I thought she was way back when I was a teenager. She had remembered me. I will never forget her.

51. **Mass in Prison**

I have attended and said Mass in many places: Yankee Stadium, private homes, churches, a tent, shrines,, hospital rooms, and picnic grounds. But no place is more upsetting to me than a prison. It is not the prisoners that I mind or the atmosphere. It is the indignity of the interrogation and search I must submit to at the front gate. Every object on my person or in a container is inspected and scanned for forbidden items.

There was a time when prisons trusted members of the clergy. Today, however, mistrust is the order of the day because so many prison visitors try to smuggle drugs, firearms, and other contraband into the hands of inmates.

On a visit to one prison, a new guard asked what was in my Mass kit. I rattled off the items: a chalice, a paten, vestments, linens, a bottle of water, a bottle containing a small amount of wine, and communion hosts—all essential for the celebration of Mass.

"Sorry," the guard said, "you can't enter the prison with an alcoholic substance."

"Good-bye," I replied, "I'm leaving."

"Wait. What about Mass?"

"If I can't take the wine in," I said, "I can't say the Mass. You can call the warden to verify what I'm saying."

He did, and he was roundly chewed out. Poor guy. He was just doing his job.

I don't blame the prison system for maintaining its security measures. The problem is the lack of trust people have for one another. It is a defense against the crime and corruption prevalent in our society.

Once past the gauntlet at this particular prison, I was directed to a recreation room to say Mass. The prisoners who attended were mostly Catholic, respectful, and extremely well behaved. I selected someone to do the Bible readings. In addition, because the prison had a large population of Spanish-speaking illegal aliens awaiting court action, I selected someone to translate my words.

In the middle of Mass, alarms and sirens began to blare and the door to the room locked automatically. Through the windows, I could see guards running to and fro with guns drawn. I heard shouting and screaming. Meanwhile, I tried to maintain my composure and continue Mass. Seeing my uneasiness, one of the prisoners said, "Don't worry, Father. It's just someone not in the proper place for roll call. This will be over in a few minutes."

I trusted this prisoner and went on with Mass. He turned out to be right.

Trust. It should be the foundation of human interaction. I hope there will eventually come a day when we don't have to conduct frisks and scans and interrogations to carry out the day's tasks.

52. Ashes for the Dead

During my fifteen years as a chaplain at Mercy Hospital in Scranton, I routinely received late-evening and early-morning calls to visit patients—sometimes to administer the Sacrament of the Sick and sometimes to carry out other tasks. Except for the lost sleep, answering the calls posed no problem for me; I had an apartment in a building next to the hospital. A bridge connected both buildings.

At about 2 o'clock one morning, I answered a call to attend a dying woman. It was Ash Wednesday, when I always carried a container with ashes. Nurses, doctors, medical technicians, kitchen workers, janitors, and other hospital staff—as well as members of patients' families—would request ashes in rooms, hallways, and elsewhere at any time of day.

Although it was very early in the morning on this Ash Wednesday, I took the container with me just in case.

By the time I got to the woman's room, she had died. Her children were still gathered around her, however, and I assured them that I had already given their mother the Sacrament of the Sick.

"We know that Mom has been anointed and was well prepared," one of them said.

Then they asked me to give her ashes, which was an unusual request, considering that she was already dead. There was no need to remind her "that thou are dust and unto dust thou shalt return." But I didn't say that to the family. Instead, I granted their request, marking the forehead of the corpse with ashes. I also gave ashes to the family members.

"Oh, thank you," they all said.

After I returned to my apartment, I thought that perhaps their request wasn't so unusual after all. Since ancient times, ashes have been given to the church "faithful," a term used to refer to church members who have received the sacraments of Baptism and Confirmation, have pledged their faith in Jesus Christ, and have accepted and abided by His teachings. The deceased woman had indeed been a member of the church faithful. The mark I had placed on her forehead was a symbol attesting to her faithfulness, a symbol that all of her children would remember for years to come. It assured them of the genuineness of her faith and would serve to comfort them whenever they thought back to her last moments. Among the words recited by a priest administering ashes are these: "Repent and believe the good news." This woman had repented, and she had acknowledged her belief in the good news of the gospels.

53. Through the Looking Glass

When I was chaplain at Mercy Hospital in Scranton, I had private quarters next door on the sixth floor of the McCauley Building. A bridge connected the hospital to the third floor of the building, making it easy for me to get to the hospital when I was called in the late evening or early morning to minister to a patient. When I returned to the McCauley building, I usually took the elevator, which ran to the fifth floor, then climbed a flight of stairs to my apartment. It was a convenient arrangement.

Next to the elevator on the third floor was a pediatrician's office with a large glass door. One day while I was waiting for the elevator with several others, a little girl on the other side of the door was fascinated by her reflection in the glass. She waved at it, primped her hair, danced, frowned, smiled, touched the image of herself, and giggled at what she saw. But when she noticed the strangers looking down at her through the glass from the other side, she got scared and ran to her mother, who was sitting on a chair across the room. Her mother opened her arms wide to scoop up the little girl. Once in the comfort and safety of her mother's arms, the little girl looked back at the adults smiling at the beauty and love we observed while she sat on her mother's lap.

I don't think there's anything more beautiful in the world than a child resting in the security and warmth of a mother's hug.

54. **A Wrong Turn That Was Right**

In 1970, the diocese assigned me to St. Mary's Church in Dunmore. The years I spent there were probably the happiest of my priesthood.

Although I was still in my twenties and had served only two years in the priesthood, the three older priests at this parish treated me like a brother and made it clear that I was their equal. Their attitude—and the kindness of the parishioners and other people in Dunmore—reminded me of what Archbishop François Fénelon, of Cambrai, France, wrote in 1699: "All humankind is but one family . . . all men are brothers and ought to love each other as such."

Msgr. Joseph Quinn, the pastor of St. Mary's, never took advantage of my rookie status but instead worked just as hard as I did. So did Fr. Bill Healy, who was fourteen years older than I. The retired former pastor, Msgr. Raymond Larkin, performed duties as necessary while he was waiting for the reopening of the Scranton retirement home for priests, Villa St. Joseph, which was undergoing renovation. He never interfered with the work of his brother priests and never offered suggestions unless he was asked. It must have been difficult for him to keep his mouth shut while he had a raw newcomer like me around.

Besides saying daily and Sunday Masses, my duties included visiting patients at four hospitals, teaching CCD classes to students from public schools, and making more than thirty house calls on every First Friday to distribute Holy Communion. There were also baptisms, weddings, funerals, and viewings. The workloads of the other active priests were just as heavy as mine.

We priests took turns presiding at funerals. There were about two every week. The priest in charge made all the necessary arrangements for the services and also attended the viewing to say the rosary.

At one viewing, an unusual development underscored Archbishop Fénelon's observation. The viewing was for a man who had died out of town. He was the head of a family. After his body was returned to Dunmore, I made the funeral arrangements. On the night of the viewing at O'Donnell's Funeral Home, I did not recognize any of the children or relatives. But that was not unusual. After all, it was a big parish, and I was relatively new to it. I told the family members that I was there to pray the rosary with them. They thanked me, and I proceeded with the rosary.

Afterward, one of the family members approached me and said, "Who are you?"

I was surprised. Surely the family had seen me at Mass or even gone to confession to me. Nevertheless, I introduced myself. Sensing that they had never heard of me, I said, "Isn't this the funeral for Mr. Smith of St. Mary's Church?" They said no. It was for Mr. Jones of St. Anthony's Church. They were expecting Fr. Tony Tombasco, of St. Anthony's, to say the rosary.

It was then that I realized how I had gotten into this embarrassing predicament. O'Donnell's had two large viewing rooms—one to the right of the front door and one to the left. I had taken a wrong turn. It reminded me of an obituary in one of my hometown newspapers, *GRIT*. It published the wrong house number for the address of a deceased person. Consequently, all the flowers and sympathy cards—as well as food and other items— were sent to the wrong address.

I apologized profusely to the family. However, they thanked me just as profusely. But there was more. The Smith family in the other room also thanked me for saying the rosary, apparently concluding that God would accept the prayers on behalf of both deceased men. I realized then that Mr. Jones was not a stranger to me. Nor was Mr. Smith a stranger to the other family. After all, as Archbishop Fénelon had pointed out, "All human kind is but one family."

Everyone laughed about the mix-up, even though it was a solemn occasion, and everyone made friends. From that day on, Msgr. Quinn, Msgr. Larkin, and Fr. Healy called me "wrong-way Cummings." In a way, though, I was right to be wrong, considering how my mistake brought so many people together. That night—in the immortal words of Yogi Berra— "I saw a fork in the road and I took it." And there was no harm done.

55. Memorable Baptisms

After I was ordained a deacon in 1967, part of my duties included baptizing children and adult converts. This experience, as well as my academic studies, made me increasingly aware of the importance of baptism.

I first administered the sacrament to an infant boy at a church in Brodheadsville in August 1967. I don't remember his name. Nor do I remember the names of most of the children I baptized in hospitals and churches after I was ordained a priest. I always thought that if I needed to know their names, I could look them up in parish records.

However, the name of one infant I baptized became forever lodged in my memory twenty-four years after the baptism took place. Here was what happened. In 1979, when I was the Catholic chaplain at Mercy Hospital in Wilkes-Barre, I was summoned to baptize a newborn having difficulty. (It is routine for a priest to be notified in instances in which a baby may be in danger of death. If there is no time to call priest, any nurse who knows how to perform a baptism according to church rules may administer the sacrament.) After I baptized the child, a boy, I conferred with the mother and other family members to assure them that the baby had been validly baptized and to answer any questions that they had. Twenty-four years later, I was having supper at the Annunciation Church Parish Center in Williamsport (now part of St. Joseph the Worker Parish) when three persons approached me: Chris Washington, who was a seminarian in the Scranton Diocese, and his parents. His mother informed me that Chris was the child I baptized during that emergency call at Mercy Hospital back in 1979. What a wonderful feeling it was to know that I was the one who baptized Chris, who today is a priest serving the diocese.

On another emergency call, one that I received when I was assigned to St. Patrick's Church in Wilkes-Barre, I was asked to baptize a premature baby at one of the local hospitals. When I entered the maternity ward, a nurse was bathing a newborn. Afterward, she led me to the premature baby and then assisted me while I baptized the child. She then called me aside to tell me that the baptism actually was not necessary, explaining that she routinely baptized all babies in the maternity ward when she bathed them. Perhaps that was not unusual in the forties, fifties, and sixties—when she was serving at the hospital—for a nurse to do what she did. It would be today.

You may be wondering whether a person can receive baptism twice. The answer is no. However, a conditional baptism can be performed if there is a possibility that the first baptism was invalid.

Many baptisms are memorable because of the behavior and beauty of the babies. Some children don't miss a thing as they observe the people hovering over them. The movements of these infants—and of course the noise they make—often amuse family members, relatives, and friends. Some infants scream bloody murder constantly, causing the baptism to be as brief as possible. Others scream only when cold water is poured on their heads. (Warm water reduces the likelihood of screaming.) Still other babies—especially those with enough hair to minimize their reaction to the water—don't scream at all. At all baptisms, there is nothing more beautiful than those little faces looking around at the surroundings.

When I was stationed at St. Jude's Church in Mountaintop, baptisms took place on just one Sunday of the month. Consequently, there were times when we priests had ten or more children to baptize. Three priests would assist the pastor in the administration of the sacrament. These were impressive ceremonies, with as many as two hundred attendees in the pews.

On one of these occasions, the newly ordained assistant was the baptizing priest. The pastor and I stood by to help him. He was large man, like a football lineman. After baptizing the first infant, he raised the child for all to see and said, "Behold a child of God!" The pastor and I were dumbfounded. After baptizing the rest of the babies, he did the same thing. The people in the pews were amazed and impressed at this unusual way of introducing the newly baptized children. I too was impressed, but I was praying that he would not drop any of the babies. I never again saw him raise a child at a baptism, but I must say he certainly got the attention of the family members and relatives on that day. I later learned that he got the inspiration for this "maneuver" from *The Lion King*, a movie in which the future king of the jungle was elevated for all the animals to see.

I baptized all three of my nephews and a grandniece and a grandnephew and loved doing it. Afterward, all of us family members enjoyed a get-together.

At the baptism that I most remember, I was a spectator. It was for my mother, a baptized Presbyterian, who converted to Catholicism in the mid-1950s. In those days, it was customary for the church to administer a conditional baptism to converts. I remember so well the look of resolve on my mother's face as she leaned over the baptismal font as Fr. Bernard Grogan, assistant pastor of Annunciation Church, performed the baptismal rite. My mother's decision to become a Catholic was a big one for her; much thought and prayer went into it. She said once that one reason she studied Catholicism and converted to it was to enable her to answer all the questions my brother and I would ask about the faith.

The Sacrament of Baptism is a sacrament of initiation. It sets us apart. It is a new reality of God's presence in our lives. We Catholics believe that baptism makes us temples of the Holy Spirit and, as such, owe every baptized Christian the honor and respect of a brother or sister in Christ.

56. The Little Girl in St. Peter's Square

Vast crowds form in St. Peter's Square in Vatican City every Easter and Christmas to receive the Pope's apostolic blessing, called *Urbi et Orbi* (*to the city and to the world*), administered from the central balcony of St. Peter's Basilica. On such occasions, the Pontiff also delivers a timely message interwoven with his Easter or Christmas greeting.

On Easter in 2016, for example, Pope Francis told the crowd in the square: "The Easter message of the risen Christ, a message of life for all humanity, echoes down the ages and invites us not to forget those men and women seeking a better future, an ever more numerous throng of migrants and refugees—including many children—fleeing from war, hunger, poverty and social injustice."

On certain other special occasions, the Pope also delivers an *Urbi et Orbi* blessing and a message. In addition, the Pope holds an audience every Wednesday afternoon in the square in good weather or in an audience hall in cold or inclement weather.

In 1982, while in Rome studying at the North American College, I joined several hundred thousand people in the square on a Sunday in a special celebration for the canonization of Maximilian Kolbe. He was a Polish priest who sacrificed his life in a Nazi concentration camp for another man who had a family. I stood far back in the crowd among people from around the world, some wearing native costumes. As we waited for Pope John Paul II to begin the Mass, a little girl of three or four came by crying and looking for her mother. Three women stooped to comfort the girl. One was wearing an elaborately decorated Japanese kimono and obi, the second was wearing a colorful African costume, and the third was wearing a Polish folk costume.

Speaking Italian, they assured the child that they would locate her mother. Nearby just moments later, they found the mother, who had a happy reunion with her daughter. The three women who came to the girl's aid must have been students attending college in Rome. To me these kindly women represented the Universal Church.

In a homily I preached after returning to the United States, I told the story of these women and mentioned that they all had spoken to the little girl in Italian. As I was greeting people after Mass, a woman told me she really liked the sermon. "But," she added, "you should have said the women were speaking in the language of love."

It was true. The women *were* speaking in the language of love, which I am sure the little girl understood in the women's faces, their gestures, and the concern they showed for her—a concern that every Christian should have for people who have lost their way.

Assumption Church in Cascade Township, Pa.
(Pastor 1981-83)

57. Thunder and Lightning

There is no greater attention-getter in nature than a powerful electrical storm. But when such a storm occurs during a religious service, it can strike the fear of God into you. For example, on Good Friday in 1981, I was conducting services at Assumption Church in Cascade Township, Pa., when dark clouds gathered and heavy rain started to fall. (Assumption, a mission church of St. Aloysius Parish in Ralston, is about fifteen miles from Williamsport.) Nothing eventful happened until the reading of the following paragraph in the Passion of Our Lord.

"Then Jesus cried out again with a loud voice, and yielded up his spirit. And all at once, the veil of the temple was torn this way and that from the top to the bottom, and the earth shook, and the rocks parted asunder; and the graves were opened, and many bodies arose out of them, bodies of holy men gone to their rest: who, after his rising again, left their graves and went into the holy city, where they were seen by many. So that the centurion and those who kept guard over Jesus with him, when they perceived the earthquake and all that befell, were overcome with fear; no doubt, they said, but this was the Son of God" (Matthew 27: 50-54).

At that moment, the sky flashed, thunder boomed, and the lights in the church went out. Everyone was stunned. I paused for a moment so that all of us could regain our composure. It was so dark that I had to use a candle to finish the prayers and other readings. Just as the congregation was dispersing, the lights came back on. On the way out of the church, people commented on how impressive—and how frightening—their experience was. No one cracked jokes, and everyone went away with a story to tell.

In another incident, an electrical storm struck while I was conducting burial services at Montoursville Cemetery for a parishioner of Ascension Church in Williamsport. The cemetery was in a nearly treeless field. A canopy over the burial site rested on four metal poles. About fifty family members, relatives, and friends stood around the coffin.

As I began the prayers, rain started to fall and everyone crowded under the canopy. Then came the lightning and thunder. The bolts occurred in rapid succession, one flash after another followed by loud cracks and booms. There we were, in the middle of an open field beneath a canopy held up by four "lightning rods."

Never in my life had I said prayers for the dead at greater speed. I was like a 45- rpm record spinning at 78 rpm. At the end, I said, "Go! Get back in your cars as fast as you can." The cemetery workers threw a tarp over the casket and ran for their lives.

Among the fifty there that day, even the most hardened sinner must have uttered a prayer, such as, "Lord, get me out of here alive!" It was a very scary moment. The Lord speaks to us in different ways, sometimes through lightning, thunder, or other natural phenomena.

58. The Polio Scare

Polio was a terrifying word for American children in the 1940s and 1950s, when I was growing up. It could disable, paralyze, or kill its victims. In the epidemic of 1952, this viral disease infected almost 58,000 persons in the U.S.

The disease was active in the summer months, when kids would see scary headlines such as: "Two More Polio Cases Diagnosed" or "Boy Dies of Polio." When we went to the movies, we would see newsreels showing children in iron lungs. An iron lung was a cylindrical metal chamber that forced air into and out of the lungs of a child with paralyzed chest muscles. The patient would lie in a bed pushed inside the chamber. Only his head remained outside. Because the disease often spread via contaminated water, children were afraid to go swimming.

Although polio (in full, poliomyelitis) most frequently infected children, it did not ignore adults. Franklin Delano Roosevelt, the thirty-second U.S. president, contracted the disease at age 39. It paralyzed him from the waist down. However, he was able to serve in the White House from 1933 to April 1945 with the aid of braces, crutches, and a wheelchair.

In 1947, when I was five years old, I began to have difficulty walking. I feared the worst: polio. When my mom took me to our wonderful family physician, Dr. Charles A. Lehman, he diagnosed me with rheumatic fever. That disease damaged my heart, but my condition was manageable. I am now seventy-five and am thankful that I remain in relatively good health even though my heart continues to require close monitoring.

But even after Dr. Lehman's diagnosis, I continued to worry that I really had polio.

In those days, there was no TV. Many children learned of important news developments about polio from theater newsreels, including Movietone News and Universal Newsreel. Seeing suffering children on the big movie screen made the disease seem more threatening than it was. (An overwhelming majority of American children never caught the disease.)

The March of Dimes, an organization formed to raise money to combat polio, sponsored movie ads requesting donations. In one ad, Howard Keel, a bass-baritone who appeared in movie musicals, sang an uplifting song—"You'll Never Walk Alone"—to stricken children. As a kid, I wondered why Keel was singing about walking to children who might never walk again. After a typical March of Dimes ad, the theater lights would come on and ushers would take up a collection.

During this time, Dr. Jonas Salk developed an injectable polio vaccine that was distributed for the first time in 1955. By 1961, the annual number of polio cases in the U.S. fell to just 161.

Fear is a powerful emotion in young children with lively imaginations. One way to ease the fear is to educate children about what they fear. But, in the 1952 epidemic, education about poliomyelitis was trumped by panic and ignorance. Would the epidemic worsen? Would more and more children end up in an iron lung? These were among the questions that occupied my mind at the time.

However, thanks to medical science and the blessing of the Salk vaccine, inoculated children were able to resume their normal lives without worrying that death or paralysis was stalking them.

59. Thanksgiving in Sicily

While in Italy on a three-month sabbatical, I found that Italians always find a way to go the extra mile—literally and figuratively. This characteristic became evident to me and my fellow priests when we traveled from Rome to Sicily on our Thanksgiving holiday.

After taking a train south to the Italian boot, we did not have to get off when we arrived at the sea. Instead, the train drove onto a large ferryboat for the ten-mile trip to the island. After we arrived, the train was divided into two sections with their own locomotives. One trundled off to Syracuse (Siracusa), on the southeastern coast, and the other set out for Palermo on the northwestern coast. We took the Syracuse train southward but only part way down the eastern coast, to Taormina, where we had arranged accommodations at an old villa converted into a hotel. The front porch sat on the edge of a cliff overlooking the Mediterranean.

Hungry after our trip, we settled in at a trattoria for a meal. A trattoria lacks the fancy décor of a four-star restaurant, but the portions are large and tasty and the service informal and friendly. Because the meal was so good, we decided to have our Thanksgiving meal there the following day. One of our group who spoke Italian asked the chef whether he could prepare a turkey with all the traditional trimmings of an American Thanksgiving dinner. The chef nixed the idea because turkeys were imported from abroad and available only in a frozen state. But he agreed to cook chickens instead.

The next evening we returned to this delightful little place, which was closed to all customers except our group of twelve. The chef served us a spectacular feast of chicken, vegetables, potatoes, polenta, and salad, along with wine, pasta, sorbet, various sauces, and a homemade cake. We must have been there for four hours, talking, singing, and enjoying our wonderful dinner in the little trattoria.

As I said before, the Italians find a way to go the extra mile, whether it's to see that their guests reach their destinations on a train that crosses water or whether it's to accommodate their guests with a meal just for them. Though we were strangers to Taormina, the staff of the trattoria made us feel special, like regular customers.

60. Arming Ourselves to Act for Jesus

Oftentimes when trying to come up with an idea for a homily, I find the answer in the most unusual places. In one instance, for example, I received inspiration from a crossword puzzle.

Every morning I do the crossword in the Williamsport Sun-Gazette. While struggling to develop an idea for the homily, the gospel passage was from Jn.15 "I am the vine, you are the branches." I began to work the puzzle and noticed that the clue for a three-letter word was *branch*. Immediately, I wrote in *arm*. This answer made me think of a true war story in which an advancing U.S. Army unit came across a bombed-out church that was completely in shambles except for the walls and an alcove with a statue of Jesus that had no arms. The chaplain then set up a table on which to say Mass for the men.

In his sermon, he made reference to the statue. "Boys, look at that statue of Jesus over there. What are we to make of it? Some of us will say that it is just a damaged statue, no more. But I look upon it in a different way. I think it is saying that you and I are the arms of Jesus in the world. It is up to us to do his work. Remember that."

When I look at all the good that people do—cuddling a leprous child, saving a life with CPR, serving meals to the needy, wrapping a Christmas gift for a special grandmother, or simply opening the door for a stranger—I realize that we are indeed the arms of Jesus in the world.

I have since used this story about the chaplain's sermon in many of my homilies. It is always well received.

61. Doing What Dad Does

Children love to mimic their parents.

When I pulled up at a stop sign the other day, I saw a father and his son shoveling mulch into a wheelbarrow. The boy was about four. After the father dumped a shovelful into the wheelbarrow, he stood by while his son shoveled in a tiny scoop.

I could tell that this loading operation would go on for a while, but I was impressed with the patience of the father. He would dump in his shovelful, then the boy would dump in his. No doubt the father was aware that he could complete the job quickly if he sent the boy into the house. But, no, he kept up the slow pace so that his son could take part—and the boy was enjoying every minute of it.

What I was witnessing reminded me of a TV commercial some years ago that focused on how children imitate their parents. A father and his little boy of about three were walking along a woodsy path when they came upon a pond. The dad picked up a stone and threw it into the pond. The boy did the same, doing his best to mimic the movements of his father. After they resumed their walk, the father stooped, pulled a blade of grass, and stuck it in his mouth like a toothpick. The boy did the same. Finally, when they tired of walking, the father and son sat down against a tree. The dad crossed his legs, and so did the boy.

After a while, the father reached into his shirt pocket, took out a pack of cigarettes, and placed one in his mouth. He lit it with a match and inhaled deeply. The boy, meanwhile, took out an imaginary cigarette, struck an imaginary match, and lit his cigarette. He sat there puffing away like his dad.

Probably if the father had sniffed cocaine or snorted from a whiskey bottle, the boy would have sniffed imaginary cocaine or drunk imaginary whiskey. Eventually, the day would probably come when the boy tried the real thing. At least that was the implication of this commercial. What would happen to him thereafter was easy to imagine.

Like father, like son.

Like mother, like daughter.

Parents need to be aware of the profound effect they have on their children.

Immaculate Conception   St. Luke Church, Jersey Shore, Pa.
(Pastor 2009-2010)

* P.S. NINE BONUS STORIES

Bonus #1 Frank P. and Nellie Farrell Cummings
Wedding + 25th Anniversary October 1894 - 1919

My grandparents, Frank P. and Nellie Farrell Cummings, celebrated their 25TH Anniversary, October 1919. Their union produced ten children. Frank P. was a teacher ten years in the local schools and then became a lawyer in 1884. He was Williamsport City Solicitor from 1903 to 1939 and was an accomplished public speaker. One Sunday morning he came home from church and grandmother asked him, "How was father's sermon today?" Not wanting to be unkind to the priest he said, "Father passed two or three good places to stop." There have been times when I realize I am rambling in my sermon and the words of grandpa come to my mind, "Charles, you've passed two or three good places to stop."

Bonus #2 Budding Artist
My Dad, Charles Cummings, was the 9th of 10 children of Frank and Nellie Cummings. When Dad was in 5th grade at St. Joseph School, his teacher, Sister Mary caught him drawing a not so flattering picture of her during class. The sister sent a note home to my grandparents requesting a parent teacher conference with them about Dad's behavior. Our grandfather went over to the convent for the conference, listened to her concerns, and assured the sister that he would talk to Dad when he got home about not wasting time drawing during class. When grandpa got home he told our grandmother about the meeting, "Nell, I assured sister we would talk to Charles about paying attention in class," and then he said, "By George Nell, the picture looked just like her."

Bonus #3 "Story in Clay"

A little boy in one of the First Communion classes presented me with the gift of a "clay chalice". This is one of the most beautiful gifts I ever received! It reminds me of my 49+ years in the priesthood. Bent by years of hard work, chipped by mistakes and sins, faded like one's health in old age, yet still standing with the Lord's forgiveness, grace and love. To me, it represents the privilege of being chosen by God to share the Priesthood of Jesus Christ.

Bonus #4 My Mom's Conversion Predicted

Charlie & Jim Cummings with our 100 year old Aunt in 1948. Aunt Kate Cummings Gesler was born in Cascade, PA in 1852 and lived & farmed there until her husband Bill's death in 1926. Kate moved to Williamsport and lived with our family. When our Mom & Dad were married in 1940, Aunt Kate, who was, at the time, 88 years old, said to Mom, "Dee, I will live to see you become a Catholic". Mom didn't think anything more about until she was Baptized a Catholic in 1954. True to her word, Aunt Kate died that week at 102.

Bonus #5 Dr. Charles J. Cummings

My Dad and I were named after great uncle Charlie who was a physician in Williamsport until his death in 1926. Dr. Charles J. Cummings practiced General Medicine for years at the corner of West Fourth Street & Mifflin Place just down the block from Saint Joe's School. When my Dad was a kid and late for school, he would stop at Uncle Charlie's office pretending to be sick to get an excuse for being late for school. Uncle Charlie would examine him, write him an excuse and tell him "You'll be fine. You have a mild case of e pluribus unum" and sent him off to school. As Dad got older and studied Latin, he realized that Uncle Charlie had been on to him all along.

Bonus #6 (Mom) Marian "Dee" Cummings (1917-2014)
I attended St. Pius X Seminary in Dalton, Pa. from 1962-68. The Second Vatican Council 1962-1965 was the news and focus of everyone's attention. There were many authors writing articles and books at that time; Xavier Rynne, Hans Kung, even Thomas Merton's views on peace and justice and others were considered a little too liberal for our seminary library.

My mom worked at the public library in my home town of Williamsport, Pa. and she was able to get any book we wanted and at a discount price. Not knowing it, she became our undercover supplier of these books. On visiting day, the trunk of my dad's Ford became the bookstore, paper bags full of contraband books. I must admit, I was an accessory; before, during and after the fact, because I took the orders, collected the money, distributed the goods and read many of the books myself. My Dear Mom – May She Rest in Peace!

Bonus #7 Elizabeth "Abby" Cummings (1895-1991)
Added to Story # 6 Aunt Abby Gift of Chalice to Fr. Cummings
Elizabeth "Abby" Cummings was the oldest of 10 children of Frank P. and Nellie Cummings, she was born in 1895. Although Aunt Abby never married, her nieces and nephews were like her children. This caring woman demonstrated her love not only on us but also a lover of animals. She bought a fish bowl containing a small turtle which she called Rosie. Believe it or not that turtle seemed to listen to Abby's voice, look knowingly at her and perform tricks that all would claim impossible. Abby

would put Rosie on the table, call to her and Rosie would walk to the edge of the table, pause, look at Abby who would put out her hand and that turtle would take a leap of faith, walk off the table trusting that Abby would not let her fall to the floor. We were all amazed to watch this circus act in miniature.

Bonus #8 Our Aunts Elizabeth Cummings & Kate Gesler
When all of the brothers and sisters had moved from the family home at 705 5th Ave. Aunt Abby and Aunt Kate Gesler, who was quite elderly, moved to an apartment on W. 4th St. just across the street from Annunciation Church. Aunt Abby loved to tell stories about all the animals the family had while she was growing up. There was Moonbeam, Bob, Handsome, and Mayonnaise. When we were growing up she had a small spaniel named Elmer (Gender Confusion – Elmer turned out to be a girl). To avoid seeing those big brown begging doggie eyes, Abby put the morning newspaper between her and the dog so she could eat her bacon in peace. Picture yourself having to eat your bacon and eggs behind a curtain of newspapers.

Bonus #9 Catcher's Mitt's Long History
In 1950 Bob Steinhilper who was sports editor of the Williamsport Sun Gazette newspaper took my dad and I into the locker room of the Williamsport's minor league baseball team. We met the team and manager who were happy that I played baseball at Maynard Little League. I told him I was a catcher for our team and he gave me a used big league catcher's mitt. I used that glove throughout my childhood, college and seminary.

While stationed at St. Mary's Church in Dunmore in 1971, one of the neighborhood boys asked me if he and his two brothers could use the glove. They took it with them and I didn't think of the glove again until 1990. The boy's mother was a nurse at the Mercy Hospital in Scranton and she asked me if I would like the catcher's mitt back. The glove now was used for 10 years before I got it in 1950, the boys got it in 1971, I got it back in 1990, 50 years of very hard ware. The glove has rested for the last 25 years in a display case of old gloves at the Little League Museum in Williamsport, not because any of us were great catchers but because the glove has survived hard use for so many years.

** Epilogue

When my brother and nephew suggested that I begin writing the homily and family stories I had been telling for many years, I was aware of the work that goes into writing. I have written innumerable sermons, reports, bulletin and parish announcements; usually written with a deadline. What I had to learn was the discipline needed just to sit down at the computer or typewriter and begin writing when there is no time or date restraint. A thousand excuses appear when it is time to write and I have used every one of them.

It took me several years to compile these stories and with each one I was reminded of five additional stories. It is like sitting down and watching reruns of movies or TV shows, remembering that time and place with fondness. My purpose was to write stories of inspiration and faith, but did not want to dwell on ridicule or criticism. It seems to me that there is enough ridicule and criticism written and spoken today to go around.

I think of the early days of my priesthood in the late 60's or 70's of being on call in a parish with no cell phone or beeper, just provide a list of the phone numbers and hope and pray you can be reached in an emergency. The rectories with a fixed over attic room for the young assistant with the promise, "We'll get you a fan, Father." Hoping to get along with the priest I was stationed with, a rare worry today since so many priests are alone in their particular parishes. Doing the bulletins on a mimeograph machine then struggling to make corrections and changing ribbons on the typewriter and get the ink off my hands. Assuring the cook that "I'll eat anything but liver". Many meals today are provided by caring parishioners interested in the good health of the pastor.

My hope is that these stories will bring a smile to your face, gratitude for God's blessings, inspiration to your life from the simple faith of so many of our brothers and sisters.

Prayers and Best Wishes
Fr. Charles J. Cummings
Diocese of Scranton, Pa.